ADOPTION
What You Should Know

ADOPTION TRUTH & TRANSPARENCY
WORLDWIDE NETWORK

"The inside story of courageous people affected by adoption."

"a poignant look at all facets of the adoption dynamic. It is a rare look at the cultural, political, emotional, and economic levels. This is a valuable insight into people's lives and livelihoods that the reader will never forget."

"This book has clearly been extensively researched and meticulously collated. The author speaks from lived experience, and therefore every page is flowing with her passion. I expected to hear difficult stories in this book, but I didn't foresee the strong historical overview of the book's presence. Starting from the Middle Ages in Europe, working through the Orphan Trains of the 19th century America, and following up to present day, this is an exhaustive look at the history of child abuse in adoption policies and those who've gained something from it."

"Must reading for social workers, therapists, and anyone interested in adoption!"

"Captivating. A MUST-READ FOR ALL."
Roelie Post, Civil Servant of the European Commission
For Expert Only: The Untold Story of the Romanian Orphans

An Eye-Opening Experience. A reading that speaks of the system of childcare over time, starting from Europe, America, Asia, and, finally, Africa today. The research examines the launch and expansion of the adoption industry and focuses on its current consequences kept in the dark of public opinion. Contains a plethora of resources and notes. Warmly recommended! It includes perspectives from families left behind."

"...incredibly necessary, and the author does a great job at conveying the information and allowing the reader to react rather than slamming her bias to the reader...."

What are Human Rights?

Human rights are rights inherent to all human beings, regardless of our nationality, place of residence, sex, national or ethnic origin, colour, religion, language, or any other status. We are all equally entitled to them without discrimination. These rights are all interrelated, interdependent, and indivisible.

Universal human rights are often expressed and guaranteed by law in the form of treaties, customary international law, general principles, and other sources of international law. International human rights law lays down obligations for governments to act in certain ways, or to refrain from certain acts, in order to promote and protect human rights and fundamental freedoms of individuals or groups.[1]

The United Nations Human Rights
Office of the High Commissioner

"Imagine, you're about to have a little one. The love that you have for that little one. Then imagine somebody outside of your family you don't even know, making claims of your little one. They don't like the way you live. They're going to take your little one by force. Imagine what the loss is. When this is not just your family but your entire community—this is its children."

Gkisedtanamoogk, University of Maine
From The "First Light" Upstander Project

Table of Contents

Given the Runaround

"Before we could form words, we only had our screams and fists."

~2015 linoprint at Darius X Studio

When I finally traveled more than 5000 miles to the adoption agency, at age 44 (and for the third time), I was a little taken aback that we, adoptees, were still expected to enter through a back alley to get to the back door in the effort to obtain adoption documents—documents that should be freely given to us because they pertain to us. On the other hand, the paying applicants and adoptive parents were invited to use the *front door* and entered where larger-than-life award-winning photos of adoptive families lined the evangelical hallway. I thought this was a little peculiar—especially since it is the lives of people adopted who are most moved by the transaction.

My sister and I even respectfully waited seven years after our adoptive mother passed away before we began to ask questions. At that time, we learned we were not citizens of the United States, as we had been led to assume during our childhoods and into our adult lives. During our first trip to Seoul, I had no idea whether or not I had any right to the details of my adoption. I offer a narrative based on this trip in my book *The Search for Mother Missing: A Peek Into International Adoption.*

Into this maiden motherland voyage, I became shockingly aware of the notion that adoption is not always a "win-win-win" for all. More than 400 Korean-born adoptees traveled to Seoul that year for an adoptee conference to celebrate and contemplate 50 years of intercountry adoption. While there, a Korean man approached me in a back alley. Gesturing, he asked me to give a note to the president of the allegedly ethical agency that had pioneered overseas adoption from South Korea starting in 1954, which eventually prompted more than 200,000 domestic and overseas adoptions. Through the searching man's rudimentary English in a later email, I learned that he was a father looking for a son who was taken for adoption.

Like other international adoptees, the agency I had been adopted through also gave us the runaround when we inquired. While in South Korea, I was told that my adoption file was in Oregon. I suspected that we weren't given the complete contents of the file as the staff chose to show us one folder, each containing partial, incomplete information instead of pulling out a set of complete folders with two separate identification numbers. Then the Oregon office said I could have my file for a fee of $400. Upon my request for my adoption documents, Molly Holt, the daughter of adoption pioneers Harry and Bertha Holt, the couple who set up the processing and placement system in South Korea, inadvertently said that the agency had just finished microfilming all records in Korea—at the same office, we had initially approached. We were not allowed to view these archives. Instead, Ms. Holt asked if I had ever imagined what my life would have been like *if I was not adopted*. This is code for, be content with what they have already told me, leave well enough alone, and even: *I should be ashamed of myself for not being more grateful.* Rather than believing everything I was told about my adoption, which was very little), I looked at circumstances from a different perspective, one that was outside of my childhood upbringing, influence, and rhetoric.

This investigation is a portrait of adoption from the *back door*—a view that no one really wants to look at, talk about, or even acknowledge, but vitally important. If you're curious, I'll show you what's been going on for the past four centuries so you can protect yourself and the people you care for.

Having been involved in the adoption community for decades, I now know that for every forever family created by adoption, another family is forever torn. I've compiled this book based on this predicament because I've also noticed that the most important people of adoption have been stigmatized and completely hidden from public knowledge. The privacy involved (or secrecy) to keep the industry open for business has shocked me to the core and motivated me to unearth its foundation. My adoption also prompted this research. For example, being the only Asian in certain scenarios, I've had questions tossed at me by curious folks, and I've always felt the need to answer for why I'm here taking up space in the great United States. People ask, "What are you? What nationality are you? How long have you lived here? Do you understand English? Do you understand Korean? Do you want to learn your language? Do you want to meet your birth mother?"

These questions have compelled me to keep digging. I wanted to give accurate answers, but the problem was that I didn't have them, and I didn't know where to start. I didn't want other adopted people to be plagued with this same lack of knowledge. As a result, I wrote a series of books that I now call "Adoption Books for Adults" along this bewildering journey. These books depict how the wants and needs of elite populations outshine everyone else, which tend to prevent us from investigating pertinent aspects of ourselves regarding our family, a nation of birth, and other essentials that have to do with our true identity. The falsifying of our identities is billed at least by the adoption industry as if for our own good and protection. But is it really? Or has it been in the facilitators' best interests?

My twin sister and I were led to believe we were orphaned and even given a "Certificate of Orphanhood" as proof of this by the pioneering reputable adoption agency in the early 1970s. No one in the adoptive family thought to question them during that era. We truly believed we came from a nonexistent family, and as a consequence, the idea to even look for biological relatives did not enter our consciousness during the first three decades of our lives. It was not until we learned that other adoptees (who were told the same thing) were finding siblings, parents, and grandparents that we began to scrutinize the motives of the facilitator. (Of course, all along they've been telling adoptees the world over not to trust our biological families and nations of birth.)

Most adopted people know that when you are raised to believe that you were orphaned, you tend to accept the scraps given to you, even scraps of information about your birth or previous life before adoption as if you were lucky to get anything at all. Most of the time, we are not supposed to ask. There is an innate knowingness that your curiosity will upset your adoptive parents who sacrificed so much to "save" you. Adoptees tend to accept whatever the agency wants to give us, and some of us do so ever so politely.

But when humanity is given only half of its story, it is unable to see its entire past. When one cannot see its past, it is difficult to move forward with ease. As a consequence, history is prone to repeat itself. And it has. In this respect, the mainstream public has only been given one side of the adoption story—narratives offered by adoption agencies, its fans, friends, and followers. However, there are those who have been left behind and remain on the backburner. These individuals need to be heard. It is exhausting to continue to burrow one's story—especially when it is meant to be heard. Those courageous enough to share have been dismissed, scoffed at, and even outright bullied. Thus prevents a broader and deeper, unified, and universal image from forming. The hope is for this book to fill in the gaps.

Since after my adoptive mother's passing, I have investigated adoption beginning with myself, then looking back into its past and forward toward its evolutionary future. I've examined it from the inside out, around the side gate to its back door. My sister and I have listened to thousands of narratives from the adult adoptee community. I've also had the privilege of gaining data from Arun Dohle, of Against Child Trafficking, and expertise from Roelie Post, a children's rights official from the European Commission.

I believe the concerns presented in this book must be acknowledged. If not, everything will stay the same, with profits taking precedence over people.

My main concern was to determine *how* children were obtained. We discovered that children are not "unwanted" as alleged by facilitators. That is industry rhetoric, a campaign tactic. And mothers and fathers (of loss) are unaware of or can't afford to retain their rights, therefore grieve over the life-long sever. Many have long wished for contact. Some felt targeted for their children and then are left behind, abandoned. No matter the nation they are from, parents all over the world feel the devastation.

> *"I want study English ! ! because, i want talking with my son. He is addaping(?) 2003`form seoul,to U.S.A.. I am waiting ... for meet, longlong time ! help me please"*

This was a written message from a Korean father who approached me in a back alley in Seoul, South Korea, in 2004. The note served as a catalyst, which led me to investigate intercountry adoption at its deepest and most universal levels.

The way of nature and the movement toward truth and transparency occurred decades ago by the first initiators of social justice—individuals seeking the truth of their existence—and nothing will stop this movement from its natural progression toward oneness. We (adopted people and our allies) hand the baton to each other and we each do what we can to unearth the way of nature.

I believe my soul's primary purpose is to inform and caution communities on the scare tactics used to lure the mainstream into the web of the practice. As much as I have struggled over the years to find, understand, organize and articulate the data into something readable, I believe the public needs to know all sides of this issue, and so I trudged ahead, day-in, day-out. My trust in the evolution and innate goodness of humanity has motivated me to keep going during the longest and most difficult hours.

Keep in mind this is a rare look into the deep cracks and crevices of the adoption practice. It seeks to answer how the practice crossed boundaries and borders and got sold to humanity, to what it is today. *Adoption: What You Should Know* unravels the practice of adoption, and acknowledges the missing pieces, revealing its devastating aftermath. If we do not stop and take notice, everything will remain the same. If we continue on the treadmill, we risk repeating history. But once we look back, we can move forward—armed with tools to protect ourselves. Until doing so, humanity remains stagnant, and there will be no progress, no growth, no evolution, no reconciliation, and no rEvolution. We will continue on the treadmill and be given the runaround by those who have permitted themselves to be in charge of *other people's children.*

I need to add that I was shocked to learn that whereas adoptive mothers tend to kneejerk react at the sight of me (e.g. pushing accusatory fingers into my chest, covering the eyes of their Asian daughters while walking by, scolding me for not being obedient even though I'm most likely twice their age), mothers (of loss) have been the most supportive when it comes to advocating for the rights of adopted people. Consequently, I invited Lorraine Dusky to write a note for this book, and she gave me more than I could have anticipated.

Lorraine has been involved with adoption reform since the mid-1970s. After writing for several popular magazines, she wrote a ground-breaking memoir, *Birthmark,* in 1979, the first in America from a mother's perspective about losing a child to adoption. More recently, she published *hole in my heart.* The book is not only a personal and unabashedly frank reprisal of the good and bad times of her relationship with her daughter over the course of 26 years but also a fount of hard data that places her story in a much broader context. Today, she manages a blog called "First Mother Forum."

Dusky also authored Still Unequal: The Shameful Truth

About Justice for Women in America and written for The New York Times Magazine, Glamour, and Ms., as well as opinion columns for numerous publications, such as The New York Times, Newsweek, and USA Today. Dusky has won numerous accolades during her writing career, including two Exceptional Merit Media Awards from the National Political Caucus for Political Analysis.

You'll find Lorraine's piece, "A Single Piece of Information," as a bonus chapter in a section of this book that covers adoptions in America. She has also graciously given another message, and I have placed her support for us on the next pages.

If we, valid members of humanity, do not shine a light on agency tactics, parents will continue to be victimized. I trust that the breadth of emotions voiced from all involved will touch readers in a way that will motivate and inspire all of us to walk in awareness. If you have not already been invited to the political discussion, I hope that by the time you finish this contribution, you will feel empowered and protected to speak about adoption from an equal rights stance.

Support from a Mother

We have come a long way in America since the early beginnings of this human rights movement: While some mothers are still in the closet, many more are more willing to go public. A whole network of search angels and search companies has found ways through some of the semi-porous documentation of birth. Reunions today are not exceedingly rare yet, for some, they remain impossible. A few hearty souls take to Facebook where they write up a placard with as much information they can and hold it up for a photograph that is then shared across the social network. Demeaning and desperate, the practice demonstrates how far individuals will go to find their missing links.

While this part of the adoption reform movement was gaining momentum, the number of infants available for adoption was declining. The harm that *closed adoptions* did to both mother and children began to leak into the public consciousness, but not without the resistance from the National Council for Adoption and from the entire adoption industry. Beginning in the 80s, *open adoptions* (in which the identities of the parties were not secret) were seen as less traumatic than the old way and, with the declining numbers of available infants, advertising *open adoption* was also used as a marketing tool to entice more women to make an adoption plan for their children.

But because adopters are the ones who pay the bills at agencies, many agencies (at their behest) have resisted true openness. Agencies advertise open adoption while the "openness" is purely at the discretion of the adopters once the ink is dry on the relinquishment papers. Enforcement of such agreements is nearly impossible and almost always out-of-reach for impoverished mothers, for adopters do have legal control of the children they adopt.

Coincidentally, the decline in available infants led to a flood of intercountry adoptions. For some prospective adopters, these had the extra benefit of eliminating any possibility of a mother returning. Corruption in many poor countries led to huge human rights abuses where adoption was concerned. Children could be kidnapped off the streets in India and end up on a farm in Iowa while a grieving family was praying for their return. South Korea, for instance, kept adoption flourishing decades after the Korean War even though many mothers and fathers did not intend for their children to be adopted. It was a profitable, flourishing business for adoption agencies on both sides of the world.

As I write this, only ten states* give adoptees the unrestricted right to a copy of their original birth certificate. In more than twenty others, legislators have built-in various vetoes that allow mothers, and fathers (if they are so named), to have their names redacted from the actual and original birth certificate. But that only covers American births, not the millions of adoptees from foreign countries who landed on American soil without a birth certificate, or the names of their original parents. Only a few, working with long-ago files, if they can be found at all, are able to reconnect with mothers and fathers, who if they are still alive, may speak a language their children do not understand or speak.

What cannot be emphasized enough is that the U.S. laws sealing birth certificates and replacing them with amended facsimiles were never written to protect the anonymity or privacy of the mothers. They were enacted to protect the adopters from interference by the mother. Records are not sealed after a child is relinquished, but after the adoption is finalized by court order. Denying adopted individuals the right to their birth certificates is a holdover from the zeitgeist of an earlier era when an out-of-wedlock birth was the cause of great scandal. They are not only a blatant misinterpretation of the laws, they are also an immoral, unethical, and unjust yoke foisted upon the adopted. Legislators who enact them insist they are protecting these women from—whom? Their own children. But what they are actually protecting, according to those who are against colonialism, imperialism and even slavery, are the rights of adoptive parents to control their children's lives all of their life. Many adoptees believe that it is a despicable, outrageous, immoral, and unjust use of power that the state then invests upon the adoptive parents to control their children's free agency and will for their entire lives. Slavery is the only other institution that gives such controls for a lifetime the free agency of another person.

To deny anyone the clear right to the accurate information of their birth is an offensive violation of a right that the rest of us have merely by being born and not adopted. The original and true certificate of birth and any and all information it contains unquestionably belongs to the individual whose birth generated it.

The essays in earlier volumes by Janine Myung Ja and Jenette Moon Ja, known as the Vance Twins, certainly brought to our attention the collective depth of loss that adoptees have endured, as they themselves did when they ended up in the United States. The essays in their first volume, *Adoptionland*, are riveting. Once I started reading, I could not look away. They followed with *The "Unknown" Culture Club*. Here Janine Myung Ja tells the story of how intercountry adoption came to be such a popular way to "build a family," but with an emphasis on the true cost involved for the children themselves as well as the families left behind. These are the stories that by custom and self-policing—lest an adoptee sounds ungrateful—are not heard often. The general assumption about intercountry adoption continues to be that the child was rescued from some terrible fate, whether it be a dirty, understaffed orphanage or a hardscrabble life on the streets.

How to stanch that convenient tale is the work of the courageous Vance Twins. Giving voice to those who could not speak at the time of their adoptions, it draws on the title from the cover art for this fifth book in their series, "before we could form words, we only had our screams and our fists."

Now they have the printed word.

Lorraine Dusky

Author of *a hole in my heart*, a memoir and report from the fault lines of adoption | Founder, Birth Mother, First Mother Forum at firstmotherforum.com

*Alabama, Alaska, Colorado, Hawaii, Kansas, Maine, New Hampshire, New York, Oregon, Rhode Island.

PART 1: ORPHAN SHIPS, 1618 EUROPE

Lost Children of the Empire

The seeds of the intercountry adoption industry began more than four hundred years ago, and its history is invisible in comparison to the long stretch of humankind. Our humanoid ancestors have been around for millions of years. We might agree that the modern form of humans evolved 200,000 years ago or so—without the help of adoption law. Empires and societies are only about 6000 years old, and development on a wide scale sped ahead from the 1800s to where we are now: The millennium, what I call Generation Connect. In these vast stretches of time, humans figured out how to survive and thrive as individuals, belonging to family units, belonging to larger communities. Communities depended on each other for strength and continued existence. Along the way, the natural way of life got interrupted by money and modern technology. Doorways to products were opened just a crack, and with these openings, access to massive amounts of manufactured goods could be obtained with an exchange of the paper dollar, the credit card, and no sooner came the online buy button. Once these tools were established, anything anyone wanted was made available. All humans had the right to buy. Eventually, the *bloodgates* were kicked open even wider: Self-control and self-discipline were thrown out the window for the right to any product at any time from anywhere, and most likely, in the now. Humans found ways to expedite nature and then harvest, package, label, and sell anything and everything.

* * *

Intercountry adoption, as we know it today, has its roots in the overseas shipment of children that began as early as 1618. Of course, there are earlier cases, but the organized shipment became routine about 400 years ago. *The Lost Children of the Empire: The Untold Story of Britain's Child Migrants* by Philip Bean and Joy Melville offers a detailed historical account of the movement which evolved into Britain's child welfare system and then expanded outward. In the beginning, British children were sent to distant parts of the Empire with the purpose of solving three problems: to populate colonies, to improve the economy, and to appear philanthropic. Several charitable organizations directed the launch of the program, first designating children as *orphans*. This massive reallocation of children is now known as The Child Migration Scheme, a private child-welfare arrangement which removed the financial burden from the state while providing cheap labor under the guise of charity, as if an early departure from the children's homes gave them a *better* life and, as luck would have it, filled settlements with good British stock. Additionally, this conveniently avoided the government's responsibility to maintain and educate its own.

Exporting children for overseas care used to be a very private affair and a surreptitious practice administered and made legal by clergy members through their connections within government. The charities in charge insisted on positivity and prayer when it came to the nefarious practice. This guidance has deterred families who have lost children to the system from obtaining any justice.

At its inception, the British authorities feared children loitering on the street would become potential troublemakers, and this prompted unconventional solutions. Under state authorization, the children typically referred to as orphans, waifs, the needy, or vagrants, were sent to Australia, Canada, America, South Africa, Rhodesia, The West Indies, and Bermuda by the Boards of Guardians who were elected by ratepayers. What the children were really doing was helping their destitute parents, but the removal of children spared UK households from high tax rates. In April 1606, James I chartered The Virginia Company, a joint-stock corporation to establish settlements on the East Coast of North America. He requested to the citizens of the town and the legislative assembly of elected representatives of the City of London, to send orphans to America, specifically to Richland, Virginia.[23]

In 1618, the first shipment, considered a success, delivered one-hundred children. The numbers of competing charities then increased and, between the years of 1800 and 1850, twenty-five aid organizations were permitted to send children to Australia.[4]

Between 1870 and 1925, great philanthropists (called *child-savers*) sparked the second era of child migration, mainly to Canada. Upwards of 100,000 British children were used as farm laborers and homestead helpers.[5] At that time it cost less to send the children to Canada than to Australia.

The third phase started in 1920. The Canadian Depression resulted in a lower demand for children. Therefore, most of the available 10,000 children were sent to Australia. "And child migrants" as they were referred to in *The Lost Children of the Empire*, "were frequently called *orphans* by the facilitators shipping them out because people's hearts are touched by orphans and they contribute funds for their welfare."[6] The authors go on to explain that one would expect that the children would be *orphans* or *unwanted street urchins* but that the vast majority were not poor or even orphans. Ignoring the parents and families and leaving them out of the discussion gave the child placement facilitators an advantage. "Some [mothers] never read the small print that gave a Home the right to send the children abroad." One man admits he was sent to Canada in 1922 without his mother's knowledge. "My mother never knew where I went to." It was his grandmother who claimed he could not be cared for, which prompted his removal from Britain. These agencies were confident that they were doing the children an enormous favor and assumed that the children had no prospects in their home countries, in this case, Britain.

If the so-called orphans remained in the country, authorities speculated that the children would become criminals as adults. "These arguments were stated so persuasively that it was clear that the children left behind would remain in a miserable, unhappy place while the children sent overseas were off to a new, shining world." Even if the child was sent to a children's home meant for temporary care, the child was labeled as *abandoned* and sent out without parental consent. "The public face of the scheme may have been directed towards the welfare of the child, but no one could deny there were advantages to the agencies sending them."

Stringent British parents scorned daughters who became unexpectedly pregnant and sent them to homes for unwed mothers governed by priests and nuns. Once there, the charities convinced the women that they had committed a grave sin against God. The administration might allow the mothers to temporarily care for their children, pending approval, but most were sold off to appropriate religious couples as deemed by authorities. The mother was simply kept nearby for the purpose of nursing until the agency found buyers.

Naive British citizens commonly dropped off their children at charities, such as Barnardo's, the Fairbridge Society, or the Church of England Children's Society, but the parents never saw their offspring again. Set up as voluntary agencies, the Secretary of State then did not need to approve the processing of each child. Destitute parents allowed the boarding homes to care for their older children, too, believing that the institution could better provide for them.

"Once a child was placed with an organization, it was responsible for them until they reached the age of majority. Each made arrangements for the children upon arrival, but there was no standard way of dealing with them. Sometimes they went to isolated farmhouses to work; sometimes they remained in orphanages, children's homes or farm schools; sometimes they went to live in families as foster children."

Different voluntary agencies or philanthropies ran this operation, sharing the common goal of transporting *good British stock* overseas. These quality children, portrayed as superior citizens (compared to the people of other nations), were alternatively feared to be potential threats if they remained in Britain. Their shipment to other parts of the world rested upon the exported child's national responsibility to colonize distant Commonwealth nations, keeping the British flag flying abroad. "The Catholic agencies summed up the attitude [about this] in 1938 as the 'great and noble project of transplanting poor children' from 'congested and unpromising surroundings' to 'strengthen and extend the Empire, to preserve and augment our Christian civilisation which is so seriously threatened at the present time, and to give poor boys similar opportunities to advance in life to those open to the sons of comfortably-circumstanced parents.'"

The individuals championing the cause were out of touch with the realities of the adoptive environments, erroneously assuming that the *orphans* received great care. The children were ill-prepared to deal with the harsh climates, neither the dry heat in Australia nor the extreme cold in Canada, compared to the more temperate climate of the United Kingdom. "Young children arrived dressed in blazers, short trousers or skirts in the middle of a Canadian winter."

Once the manufactured orphans arrived, they grieved: "As soon as we got outside we realized how bitterly cold it was, so we all huddled together because we had no suitable winter clothing – there were no extra robes or anything like that. So we went three miles in the bitter cold and the rain and the sleet."

Boarding home inspectors might visit the Canadian farms on an annual basis, "but it was very easy for the farmers to cover-up matters [of abuse] if they wished."

"Most organizations believed it was better to cut off the children from [their] previous 'deprived' life, but the scars remain[ed] into adulthood – particularly the desperation to find any kind of family."

Annie Smith arrived from Birmingham, England, to Canada in 1928. She vocalized what many younger people adopted as children have felt. "When you are young and go out to another country, the country is strange, the people are strange, the customs are different, and you do not know what to expect; it's all-new, and you don't know what to make of it. You are at a disadvantage. And so many times you think, 'I have just got to make the best of it. I'm here and can't go back.' Home was across the Atlantic Ocean."

In 1913, Florence Aulph was told that she was going to Dr. Barnardo's Home for Crippled Children in order for doctors to straighten out her leg. After that, she expected her parents to retrieve her. Instead, without notice, Florence was shipped overseas to Canada at the age of twelve. "I was simply devastated. I never saw my mother again." She was not an orphan. She had memories of sitting next to her father in a little rocking chair and keeping him company as he tried to recover from tuberculosis caused by working in coal mines.

Adults sent away as children relayed stories of being taken down to the docks by horse-drawn carriages, boarding enormous ships, and then being dreadfully seasick while crossing the ocean. The voyage would take almost a month.

Only two or three adults supervised over 200 children. They landed in Québec, and from there they went by boat to a large children's home where hundreds of other boys and girls lived. From there, Florence was given a choice to live on a farm or in the city. Regrettably, she chose the farm. Her guardians tried to adopt her, even making a request to her mother, but were denied: "No way, you took her to Canada, but you still don't own her." Florence disclosed feelings of being withdrawn and full of resignation. "But what was the difference? I never saw [my British] mother again."

Charles Davenport was told that his mother was dead and, as a consequence, sent to Canada. He "accepted this without checking, unaware that there was such a thing as a death certificate" and later learned that she was alive, despite the story told to him by the clergy.

Another child felt bitter at being "shipped 6,000 miles away from his English home" and at his lack of access to records. Years into adulthood, he learned that even his date of birth was incorrect. Originally from Birmingham, England, "the next thing I knew, I was on a boat to Canada. We were just like cattle. When you are seven, you don't really comprehend what is going on," he left with a group of twenty children—also labeled as orphans—on the Duchess of Atholl, a 20,000-ton British steamship which carried more than 500 passengers and ported in London on its way to Halifax, Nova Scotia. From there, a photo was taken of him at the Fairbridge Farm School where he stayed. The children were then shepherded by train for three or four days, by ferry, and, finally, by bus to the school. He remembered the hundreds of waving and cheering students at the time. "I guess I took it as an adventure more than anything else, but my most startling experience was all those little kids yelling. I remember thinking, *where* am I?" He did receive a short version of his birth certificate on his twenty-first birthday, and from it learned that his birthday was documented differently than it actually was.[7] After obtaining partial records, he concluded that they must have withheld some records, "but we were not privy to them at all. It was a closely guarded secret."

Empty Cradles

"It is proposed that the Commonwealth seek out in Britain and Europe, in each of the first three post-war years, at least 17,000 children a year (i.e., about 50,000 in three years) suitable and available for migration to Australia..."

~From a Statement by the Acting Australian Prime Minister, December 1944.

The Child Migration's third phase, in which the children's lives were under the control of the religious and government authorities, began in 1920 and lasted until 1967. Until this time, as many as 130,000 children, mostly between the ages three and fourteen, had been shipped from Britain to Australia, New Zealand, Canada, or the United States on the facilitators' habitual promise of a better life. Still, in this final phase, the children's parents remained in-country and were not told that their children had been shipped permanently overseas. Despite coming from actual families, the children were led to believe they were abandoned and presented with deportation as if they were gaining *opportunities*, being *rescued*, or going on *vacation*. Then the charities *legally* processed the children as *orphans*.

Empty Cradles, by Margaret Humphreys, published by Doubleday in 1994, and the movie based on the book, *Oranges and Sunshine*, showcase the author's seven years of social work and her inadvertent discovery of the Child Migration Schemes. The fallout for these children as they matured into adults and then became elders are identical to narratives of adults adopted as children today (despite minute differences in their origins). The universal impact, however, has only recently begun to be explored. Credit is given to the Internet for leveling the playing field when it comes to publishing and the dissemination of information. In the past, only certain authorities (such as religious leaders, affluent consumers, or the elite) had the funding for accessing pertinent data, creating a limited and secretive structure. Due to the recent truth and transparency demanded by those most affected, the adoption industry is imploding. In the case of the mass migrations of children, influential churches and religious charities relocated the youngsters as far as 16,000 miles away from home and then, based on antiquated laws, prevented them from retrieving pertinent information about their personal origins. As a consequence, the children remained in the dark about their families who were left behind.

Amongst archives in England and Wales, Margaret Humphreys pieced together evidence proving that the parents of the exported children were, in fact, alive, yet their children referred to as *orphans*. Mothers and fathers revealed that no one informed them that their children had been sent out of the country; many were lied to. One manufactured orphan, by the name of Syd, told Margaret: "[My father] didn't know we were going to be sent to Australia... They did it without telling anybody. I'll never forgive them for that."[8]

The religious authorities and charities staunchly believed that they needed to correct the *dangers of society,* and these children became their easiest targets. Bureaucrats portrayed them as *needy* or *at-risk* youth and "victims of poverty, illegitimacy, broken homes, these children were regarded as 'deprived' and considered a burden on society." Humphreys added the obvious fear of society during that time, "they [so-called orphans] would grow up to be thieves and hooligans and probably finish up in jail."[9] In the same paragraph, Humphreys pointed out another palpable benefit to sourcing out children. "In the last century, local authorities found it was costing them £12 a year to support a child in a parish workhouse, whereas for a single payment of £15 they could send them overseas and be absolved of any further financial responsibility."

Those involved, including the major child care agencies and charities from the United Kingdom, offered no respect to (or even proper acknowledgment of) the poverty-stricken mothers and fathers. The statements implying that they were abandoned and had no other family members made the children feel cold and empty.

Staff handed out clean and dressy Sunday's best attire, which was horribly inappropriate for the lengthy journeys. The orderlies gave *good news*, convincing the children to expect that they would be well taken care of wherever they were headed. Vintage black-and-white snapshots depict groups of children in celebratory moods approaching the extradition from their home countries.

"I thought I was going on a holiday. They told me I was going on holiday. Said I would be away for six weeks. I didn't know where Australia was."[10]

"Mother Superior said that I had been chosen, that it was a wonderful opportunity, not some kind of punishment. But that night in bed, I cried. I was so frightened of leaving the only home I'd ever had, of leaving my school friends, my sisters, of leaving my best friend, Pearl, and never seeing any of them again."

The government authorities at the time asserted that the "opportunities for children were better in Australia." Monsignor George Crennan, a former director of the Australian Federal Catholic Immigration Committee, became involved with the immigration schemes in 1949 offered no empathy. When asked if he felt any responsibility for the displaced children, he said, "Most certainly not." Instead, he deflected questions to the Crusade of Rescue Agency, the organization which had sent the children away.

The director responded arrogantly to Ms. Humphreys,

steadfastly replying that he felt no responsibility for [the children]. The age-old adage, "I would venture to suggest that if these people had remained in England, they might not have made such progress. They would have become bell boys and other such things...." He, instead, placed the responsibility on the nations that farmed out their citizens.

The children reported how strange they felt on the ocean liner. The staff bundled the groups together and then separated the boys from the girls (and even split up siblings). "The culture shock couldn't be greater."

Other children from Ireland and Scotland joined the voyage. The children befriended each other but, soon after, were separated from their new friends. The ocean liners stopped at ports without telling the children where they were headed (or where they might be placed). The Catholic nuns and attendants removed the children at certain destinations and then just moved on to the next. These children thought that they had done something wrong, and, ultimately, blamed themselves. They believed that they were *unwanted*.

Once in Australia, the new arrivals were stunned by the scorching heat and then traumatized by their isolated placements on the new continent. A lone school and church building in the middle of nowhere surrounded by brown shrubs, long dirt roads, and scarce resources replaced England's townhouses, busy streets, and blossoming flowers spilling out of boxes.

Some of the girls were assigned to work in the laundries surrounded by large machines. The boys were forced to provide hard labor, sometimes constructing stone convents with their bare hands, and were punished with sticks and belts if they did not abide by the *Godly rules* imposed on them.

Both boys and girls reported severe abuse, either in the private seclusion of farming homesteads or public humiliations in the institutions. One girl reported being raped inside the adoptive home, but authorities accused her of being at fault for not being *grateful* enough.

Even as youngsters, the children understood that the charities and churches were completely self-congratulatory, ignoring the pain and suffering that they inflicted on others, and never acknowledging the trauma adoption caused. Margaret's friend came to the following conclusion: "These people [facilitators] enjoy patting themselves on the back... They're proud of what they do."[11]

The last child was sent out as recently as 1967, but the child welfare system shifted into what is now known as *Mother and Baby Homes* (or hospitals) that were set up in Europe, Canada, and Australia. The attitudes toward unmarried mothers improved very little, according to mothers from the Baby Scoop Era, as adoption was still a culturally acceptable form of *child protection*. The Magdalene Laundries of Ireland was still in operation until 1973. Canada refers to the practice of "scooping up" children from the First Nations People and placing them into adoptive homes (or Indian residential schools) as "the Sixties Scoop," which began in the 1960s and continued into the late 1980s.[12] In the United States, Native Americans recently held an inquiry into the seizure of their children by welfare workers (which was the norm in North America through the 1960s and into the late 1980s).[13]

From the pages of *Empty Cradles* and *The Lost Children of the Empire*, the deception that these children experienced was palpable. Those who experienced it spoke of waiting for someone (their mother or father, another family member, or authority from Britain) to arrive and help them. Even as senior citizens, many remain emotionally wounded, still waiting for some kind of acknowledgment. Starting in the 1980s, Margaret Humphreys led a small weekly discussion group for adult adoptees in Britain. A few people joined, mainly wanting to obtain their original birth certificates, but the discussions typically lasted much longer than originally scheduled.

Margaret noticed that the group was torn between upsetting their adoptive parents by investigating their own backgrounds versus remaining complacent. Before they began to search, many of these individuals waited until late in life (or until their adopters were dead). Margaret wrote that she served as not just an observer, but as an informal supporter for this group of people desperately seeking answers. The conflict between these two identities, as one adopted person said, created "enormous levels of anxiety which can dominate every waking hour." Moreover, if their parents were successfully found, there was an immense fear of rejection. Several individuals adopted from Europe spoke of the bitterness of being abandoned and also voiced their collective frustration at not being properly acknowledged.

The child migration program only ended fifty-five years ago, and most Australians remember it as a charity that served *needy* children. International adoption continues to this day. The practice has become a standardized route to obtain children in the United States due to the misinformation about the results. The simplistic, one-sided attitude that fabricated the system has barely changed over time. It has taken decades for the harm and emotional damage to be acknowledged, but religious authorities continue to deny any wrongdoing (as expected).

Help for victims can be found on Margaret's website: *ChildMigrantsTrust.com*. She has started a program called the Family Restoration Fund (FRF), which "reunites former child migrants with their families so that they can build relationships, be involved in significant family events, or urgently visit relatives in times of crisis, such as serious illness or death. The Department of Health provides its funding as part of the UK government's support to former child migrants. The Fund is open to any former child migrant sent before December 1970 from England, Northern Ireland, Scotland, or Wales as part of child migration schemes."[14]

A Romanian Mother Waits

"Poverty is no reason to take children away. Poverty is not a disease and international adoptions are not a solution. If on top of everything else, people lose their children it only worsens their overall situation."

Roelie Post, Official from the European Commission and author of *For Export Only, the Untold Story of the Romanian 'Orphans'*

In the 2009 documentary, "Child Wanted, Cash Paid – The Adoption Lobby,"[15] Marineta Ciofu, a mother, retrieves water from a well and lives in a house without electricity in Romania's northeastern province, one of the poorest regions of the small country. The nearest town is a four-hour walk away. She is married and also raising three sons. She refers to them as her "entire wealth," however, she has not seen her daughter since the girl was two-and-a-half years old.

"Who is this family that has taken my child?" Marineta asks after being handed adoption release paperwork, documents she struggles to comprehend. "How can you just take children from a home? They must have thought nobody would ask questions."

A letter from the Director-General discloses that Marineta's daughter was *legally* sent to the United States and worse: "By [adoption] law, you [the mother-of-loss] may not know the name of the adoptive family."

Roelie Post, an official from Brussels, attempts to console her after the young woman receives the news. From 1999 to 2005, the European Commission placed Ms. Post in charge of the "Romanian Orphan" dossier. Today, Ms. Post, author of *For Export Only: The 'Untold' Story of the Romanian Orphans*, knows all too well how the mass movement of children hurts families in the long run.

The astonished Romanian woman studies the words on the documents, trying to grasp the permanency of her loss. "Did [the adoption facilitators] not leave anything behind? Some paper? How can anyone take away a child without my signature?" She asks, "So if you have no money, you lose your child?"

Ms. Post, an expert on children's rights, has seen first-hand how fierce special interest groups upset and traumatize the mothers, the fathers, and the families who are left behind. The power and influence of the lobby have also threatened Ms. Post's efforts to protect children from being unnecessarily adopted.

When Marineta is told her daughter was sent to America, she is further shocked. "What? The child was sold for money?"

The agenda-driven facilitators who have pushed to legitimize the practice at the highest levels of government worldwide have even damaged Ms. Post's professional career. When one considers the correct interpretation and implementation of the United Nations Convention on the Rights of the Child (UNCRC), taking children for adoption strips parents of their children before they are given a chance to love and care for their offspring. The scheme also ignores the human rights treaty and, instead, permanently separates siblings in both the immediate and extended family.

Ms. Post's research thesis, "The Perverse Effects of the Hague Adoption Convention," and the investigational work she has done for Against Child Trafficking (ACT), have worked to reunite families. They continue to monitor, report, and legally represent families of adoption loss. However, the determined push of the adoption lobby, armed with the singular agenda of servicing their clients, keep the global gateway open, even as mothers from around the world have had their children taken unethically (in circumvention of the UNCRC).

From the very beginning, adoption has been sold on the wistful idea that the children are given to *better* families and go on to *cosmopolitan* lives and that it does the child no good to learn the truth about his or her origins. Yet, the mother in this documentary cannot be consoled with such simplistic answers. It is evident that she is, in fact, not fine without her daughter. She stands in disbelief, staring down at the legal papers.

When asked if Marineta tried to get her child back, she is emphatic, "Yes. Yes. Yes!" However, the guard at the gate of the children's home refused her entrance. She was only permitted into the courtyard where she could catch just a glimpse of her daughter on a distant balcony.

Marineta had once been told that the little girl had been sent to another school, but they did not give her any other details. Human rights activists, who are typically former orphans themselves, now wonder if this was a strategic method used by profiteers to conveniently strip parental-rights from poverty-stricken mothers and fathers? *Yes.* "Tactics such as relocating children to make it impossible for parents to visit them is a trick used by traffickers to gain access to abandoned children through official channels,"[16] a reporter wrote in *The Atlantic Times*, a German-language newspaper.

Marineta baptized her daughter "Mihaela," and her birth certificate is the only possession she has that provides proof of her motherhood. Her poverty, however, prevented her from being able to afford the travel expenses needed to visit her daughter. To this day, Marineta does not understand why she is no longer considered the girl's mother. The resistance from the children's home was too much for her.

While she admits, "I [will] think about her until [the day] I die," the adoption lobby fights forcefully to expedite foreign adoptions. Facilitators routinely demand less red tape. Most do so by claiming that they are on a crusade. Some have the audacity to claim that they are *uplifting children* and *strengthening families,* such as Holt International, a leading facilitator.

Mothers like Marineta, both past, and present, have been discarded and marginalized. Laws are passed to send children overseas to paying clients, but there is rarely help, nor any political aid for families torn apart by adoption, and in the West, there are no laws to protect parents against adoption trafficking (because most people are completely unaware of the problem). Only a few proponents from grassroots human rights organizations, like Arun Dohle of Against Child Trafficking, offer assistance for the families left behind.

Adoption is a billion-dollar industry, and as the saying goes, ignorance is bliss. Whoever wants to be told the harsh truth? It takes courage to share the bad news privately, but even more to share it publicly. The perception of adoption as an extreme form of altruism and charity is so strong that the uninformed public often persecutes and demonizes anyone courageous enough to criticize it. Therefore, the controversy remains suppressed by the mainstream media. Any unscrupulous adoption case is derided as *isolated,* or as an *irregularity,* and ignored. If this continues, thousands of children from around the world are at risk of being unnecessarily separated from their biological families into the foreseeable future.

In other industries, when unethically sourced products are revealed, it is grounds for public boycotts. However, when it comes to children's lives, not so much.

* * *

Most United States citizens remember the report on *20/20* given by John Upton called "Discovery of Romanian Orphans." This and other reports in the 1990s caused a spike in demand for children from the tiny nation. These international broadcasts prompted a flurry of flights to Romania. Numerous couples descended upon the Eastern European country, returning with a Romanian *orphan* to show off to their respective congregations.

The imagery of abandoned babies and toddlers idling in cribs with malnourished bodies and vacant eyes staring off-camera motivated countless individuals to put in an application for a foreign child. The *adoption option* fervor seemed justified. It was rare to hear anyone speak out against the adoption of *destitute* children. To voice concern against the campaign to *save the orphans* would have been construed as totally unreasonable, ludicrous, even. There was vicious pressure to step up the intercountry trade in vulnerable human beings by special-interest groups because of the enormous income potential for facilitators.

Because Romania's economy could not support the country's population growth, numerous parents placed their children in orphanages for what they believe was *temporary care*. Between the years of 1990 and 1991, however, facilitators exported 10,000 children overseas. Roughly 30,000 Romanian children were taken within a ten-year period. The problem, at least to reform activists, was that "most of [the Romanian children] were not orphans."[17]

Agencies made arrangements with these orphanages, sending children to France, Italy, Israel, and to the United States by the hundreds. Romanians seeking to adopt, in contrast, did not stand a chance because they could not afford the expenses involved. Americans, however, could pay the $30,000+ in fees for a child. Multiplied by 30,000 applicants, that amounted to a turnover of roughly $900 million. In 2006, the former director of Romania's adoption authority, Theodora Bertzi, said that this number was "not exaggerated."[18]

Since the 1990s, agencies have processed over 250,000 overseas children. (This figure does not include children adopted domestically.) Romanian adoptee (and contributor to the *Adoptionland* anthology), Georgiana Macavei, has much to say about the fervor to adopt. The gist of her narrative is that *she was not an orphan*, but she was, nonetheless, taken from her family. Like many intercountry adoptees aware of the crisis, Macavei must now try to undo the damage and rebuild relationships with her siblings spread out across the world, which is difficult. Rarely do adopters support any efforts of this kind. In fact, they tend to disparage any contact whatsoever.

Many adult adoptees are unwittingly used to serve as

adoption poster children giving the impression that only *positive* stories exist. In reality, the system abandons mothers and decimates the native communities that they are claiming to help.

With the best of intentions, prospective clients (called *adoptive parents* on agency websites before they pay the application fee or obtain approval) want to save orphans. Because of the photos and videos of gaunt children in the media, adopting from Romania appeared to be the *right* thing to do. The market, of course, continues to flourish rooted by such assumptions.

* * *

As was the case with Marineta Ciofu, when many Romanian mothers return to orphanages for their children, they are shocked to discover that they are simply not there. Without parental knowledge or consent, the children have already been sent abroad. Forged documents made the process *legal,* and parents were told that they could not see them. "Stolen children, or children with a falsified identity, could be legally adopted under the Hague Adoption Convention."[19] This international agreement professes to *protect and safeguard* as if sending children overseas is *in the best interests of the child.* However, lobby groups pushed the convention to benefit *intercountry adoption* without consideration for native families, tribal communities, or to the nations forced to export their citizenry. Moving children from one location to another made it easy for facilitators to legally gain access to *"abandoned"* children. As a consequence, the lucrative process, riddled with corrupt and dishonest administrators, lawyers, bureaucrats, and social workers, completely ignores the human rights of those most affected.

Today, adoption is considered as American as apple pie, at least in the United States. The idea to simply apply for adoption seems to be well ingrained into the Western psyche. Hearing about *starving children in need of loving homes* is as commonplace as going to church on Sundays, but no one talks about the mothers or the families left behind. Why is that? Is it because of the west's love affair with adoption?

The Love Affair with Adoption

The adoption lobby says:

> *"Every child has a right to [']a['] family."*

Before the Permanent Bureau of the Hague Conference formed a legal structure that concentrated *on how to process children for foreign adoptions* that are (allegedly) made "in the best interests of the child and with respect for his or her fundamental rights," a human rights treaty, called the United Nations Convention on the Rights of the Child (UNCRC), had previously established special rights for children. As the only nation that did not ratify the UNCRC, the United States, instead, invited certain organizations interested in intercountry adoption (adoption agencies, including Holt International, non-governmental organizations, almost 70 government officials) to improve the industry. The committee hoped to prevent the abduction and sale of trafficked children, but the result is now the Hague Adoption Convention (HAC), a co-operative legal construct that processes children for export and import. The HAC promotes the practice from the demand side. The players did not invite organizations or persons who might be critical of adoption, such as parents, families, indigenous groups, trafficked adopted people, or other victims exploited by the system. And most of us have been exposed to the "right to adopt" rhetoric. Nothing was ever said about rights to our family. The idea of helping impoverished families had already been rejected in adoption law.

Adoption agency representatives refused to engage with small nations that advocated for less severe forms of care, such as kinship (from immediate or extended family members), temporary care, foster, or community care. They did not take into account that some parents used orphanages to provide brief short-term shelter for their children and that a great many of these parents were not informed about the risk that their children could be matched with strangers overseas. Instead, the lobby groups fought to ensure that adoption would become a priority. Previously acceptable methods of care could then be bypassed with this new and so-called *safe passage*. As a consequence, by promising a *safe structure* for the youngest citizens of other nations, more children could then be made available for overseas adoption.

On the surface, The Hague Adoption Convention on the Protection of Children and Co-operation in Respect of Intercountry Adoption (HAC), otherwise known as adoption law, might appear to be in the best interest of the child: "Recognizing that the child should grow up in a family environment, in an atmosphere of happiness, love, and understanding." However, it is not. Unlike the United Nations Convention on the Rights of the Child (UNCRC)—intended to be a human rights treaty, the HAC was built as if adoption is child protection. It promoted sending children overseas—which was demand-driven and lucrative—before the alternative, less permanent and invasive forms of child welfare could be considered by the parents of the so-called *available* children.[20]

The problem is that innocent parents were being classified as unsafe or inadequate *before* they committed any crime, particularly against their children. This meant almost anyone could be deemed *unfit* to parent, and any *wanting adopter* could win a bid for a child after a brief home study. A family's poverty was used as the legal justification for this, and as a consequence, children were made unnecessarily available for the market. Economic superpowers could afford to pay the exorbitant fees while the citizens from small nations could not. Although the HAC was supposed to protect children, it was written *in co-operation and respect for international adoption*, but it did not recognize children's rights. The legal framework did not address pressing issues, such as offering emergency phone numbers for children who did not understand the long term consequences of the act, accountability for unethically obtained and trafficked children, or for those who were sent to abusive households. The system was built solely for the benefit of the receiving parties. The final language was approved in 1993, and it became enforced in May of 1995. Beginning in April of 2008, the United States became a full member of the HAC, and the provisions it outlined governed the practice between itself and other nations.[21] It claims to protect *birth parents* (as well as all others involved in the adoption process), yet the handbook on implementation provides no recourse for adopted people to obtain their rights to their families, nor does it provide funding for parents to find their children. It is based on agency advertising efforts and the false premise that parents and families do not exist, which perpetuates the stigma that children are *unwanted* or *orphaned*.

I remember when adoptees were told through the social media grapevine to advocate for the Hague Adoption Convention as if it served us. I suspect that stakeholders initiated that campaign and their customer base consisting mainly of adoptive parents and congregational members. During the same time, Child Rights expert, Roelie Post, of Against Child Trafficking spearheaded investigations and monitored facilitators. Ms. Post's research paper, "The Perverse Effects of the Hague Adoption Convention," in addition to the subsequent findings from her associate, Arun Dohle, the investigator behind the "Inside Story of an Adoption Scandal," and "Fruits of Ethiopia - Intercountry Adoption: The Rights of the Child or the 'Harvesting' of Children?" were ignored by the adoption community but convinced me to shift my point of view on the industry.

Facilitators, speaking on behalf of *orphans,* claim that children want a *permanent home*, but permanency allows agencies to simultaneously gain public approval for the practice while completely ignoring the rights of children—even as adults. Adopted people have the most problems with this verbiage: "the child's right to *a* family." This right is combined with a child-welfare strategy to send children to *permanent* homes. In reality, *permanency* means absolutely no legal means for future contact with one's own family. Ever. *Permanency* places a restraining order upon the adopted individual from vital members of his or her family, including mother, lineage, and ancestry. Instead of protecting families, special interest lobbying groups focus efforts on making certain that the intercountry adoption pipeline remain open.

The worst-case scenario is evidenced by the case of "Masha" who was adopted from Russia to the United States by a divorced man who claimed, during his home study, that he wanted *a daughter* to replace the one his wife had taken custody of and with whom he rarely had visitation rights. He adopted Masha with the help of adoption experts and professionals from the Joint Council on International Services (JCICS). The case against Masha is an example of how the most horrible abuse is still ignored by the industry—even against non-minorities. Her situation made the news, but the cases of children of color have barely warranted attention in the past. The trade association, located in the United States, had set the standard for ethics in adoption for forty years but has since closed its doors after being subjected "to the same trends that have impacted many of our partners over the last decade" that bankrupted the organization.[22] Adult adopted people, and human rights activists are thrilled that JCICS is no longer in business. When the six-year-old girl arrived at the adoptive home in 1998, she was made to sleep in the same bedroom with divorcee Matthew Mancuso, her newly-assigned *father* whose ex-wife had custody of their biological daughter. Whereas the home study described Mr. Mancuso as a "caring, loving man who misses the parenting role that he had with his [biological] daughter" and "highly moral," he repeatedly raped the [adopted] girl and posted pornographic images of her on the Internet for the next five years.[23]

Most shocking has been the adoption community's reaction to "Masha's" case. It has become evident that profits are placed above people as Masha had stated in her Congressional testimony that, when she told her story publicly, "all the adoption agencies, not just Matthew's, tried to cover [it] up." Adoption profiteers feared the story could result in a "potential negative impact on international adoption." *Did they mean a potentially negative financial impact?* In other words, *staying positive* actually ensures adoption abusers to escape accountability, resulting in further abuse.[24] Further abuse is highlighted in my forthcoming investigation called *Adoptionized: An Orphan's Critique of the Evangelical Orphan Movement.* Which begs the question: Why are these agencies still allowed to self-monitor and to self-police when they have proven themselves, time and again, incapable of any sort of self-regulation?

The biggest fear for the adoption profiteers is being accused of child trafficking. Agencies must preserve their reputations, so they use the protection of *positive* and *successful* stories to hammer home their message that all adoptions are *good* for their businesses to survive, grow, and thrive. The deaths and plethora of abuses against adopted children, as a consequence, have been ignored. For crimes to be hidden, the adoption must be seen as inherently good. This scheme has worked, at least in Masha's case. Despite the torturous abuse that she endured, profits were made, and the industry still maintains a pristine reputation.

For the last century, industry administrators have denied any trauma caused by the practice. One of the most recent strategic moves to keep profits up has been a push for *open adoption.* The client promises to report on the child's progress and send photos to the ousted mothers. In an open adoption, the child is, at least, permitted to know that his family of origin exists. Again, however, when parents are asked about this system, they report that it has failed the families separated by it. The child, used as a pawn, is caught between two families: one is legally protected, while the other is not. As an adult, the adopted person copes with conflicting emotions and is forced to choose between one family over the other, resulting in feelings of guilt or shame if they show favor.

Despite this turmoil, those mining the field cannot imagine placing a moratorium on the practice. They believe, through reform and refinement, that moving children here or there can only get better. The Hague Adoption Convention may appear to be a viable instrument for safeguarding human rights, but it, instead, has allowed for agencies to ignore the United Nations Convention on the Rights of the Child and created a fully-sanctioned pathway that permanently alters the natural-born right and God-given dynamic of genetic ties.

You will read later on how adoption profiteers accused those who placed value on the natural family unit as having an *infatuation with blood-ties*—as if this was a bad thing. This was the prevailing allegation against anyone in Asia who had the audacity to argue against the influx of the resolute child saviors. This, along with racist attitudes and lies against Asians, fierce proselytizing efforts made by evangelicals, and lack of access to information, are the contributing factors to the reason citizens of nations big and small could not protect themselves against a flourishing and private child market.

PART 2: ORPHAN TRAINS, 1854 AMERICA

The Emigration Plan

"Kind men and women who opened their homes to one of this ragged regiment would be expected to raise them as they would their natural-born children, providing them with decent food and clothing, a common education, and $100 when they turned twenty-one. There would be no loss in the charity, Smith assured his audience. The boys were handy and active and would soon learn any common trade or labor. The girls could be used for all types of housework."

From Orphan Trains: The Story of Charles Loring Brace and the Children He Saved and Failed, Pg. xv by Stephen O'Conner

There was a time in the history of the United States when Protestant and Catholic missionaries in New York could obtain children from impoverished immigrant families from European backgrounds and send them to live on rural farms in the West and in the Midwest. These children, of Irish, German, Italian, Russian, and Austrian descent (among other ethnic groups), never saw their families again. Many children received punishments from the people with whom they were matched with and internalized the turmoil. As a consequence, no one knew (or thought) to set up assistance for these children, leaving them isolated in the new homes and without contact information in case of an emergency. Most could do nothing but suppress their painful experiences, not knowing that so many others were sent on the same trans-continental expeditions.

Charles Loring Brace was born June 19th, 1826, to a well-to-do Connecticut family.[25] After traveling in Europe, he became aware of a practice by which charities matched children with families other than their own, now known as the Child Migration Schemes. In autumn of 1848, Brace returned to New York, studied theology at Yale University, and then, at the age of twenty-seven, founded the Children's Aid Society in 1853.[26] Other influential men from surrounding districts met to discuss the formation of an association, but they recommended Mr. Brace to take the year-long head position. Because Brace foresaw that the job might distract him from his studies, he wrote to his father about his trepidations. However, he soon realized missionary work could be more useful than that of a pastor. He decided to accept the city missionary position. He organized city-wide meetings, networked with the clergy and the press, wrote, and preached.[27]

A barefoot nine-year-old girl further motivated Reverend Brace. On May 19th, 1854, the two crossed paths when she asked him for money. While giving the girl a loaf of bread, it dawned on the Reverend that farmers needed laborers, and the idea struck that he could employ street children as apprentices and hired hands. The girls could be used for household chores and the boys as farmhands.

"He believed that America's Christian farmers would welcome the homeless children, not only give them work, but treat them as new sons and new daughters. He imagined sending tens of

thousands to the country. [28]

After seeing the children loitering New York, it was impossible for him not to feel responsible for them. He first networked with asylums and institutions to care for the children with the proposal to "drain the city of this class by communicating with farmers, manufacturers, or families in the country who may have need of such employment." Circulars and letters from the Children's Aid Society announced that the movement would "have its share of Christian liberality," including Sunday meetings and, ultimately, being good influences in the children.

The children began arriving in droves, and the money poured in. Brace wrote to one of the trustees: "We had some four hundred dollars sent in, part in cash, without the trouble of collecting." [29] Boys were given jobs, the first being shoemaking, and they won public attention.

As with most new ventures, Brace needed to bring in additional funds. He endeavored to raise money for a bigger staff, thus deciding to "let residents simply pick out the child they wanted for themselves." He made schedules, raised funds, and obtained permissions from various authorities to make his vision possible, calling it *the Emigration Plan.* [30]

"Brace and his staff of volunteers visited orphanages and reformatories and the homes of impoverished parents," searching for children to recruit. The intent of the program became the basis of foster care as the children were not legally stripped of their names, although this sometimes occurred. Many of the children were given the surnames of the foster families and/or given a new first name, which altered their identities and made the placements much like adoption. It wouldn't be until decades later when adoption lobbyists would propose *permanency* as if a good thing that children desired. Even at this point in the evolution of the experiment, the little ones were expected to act as if they were the farmer's real children.

In agrarian states, Brace published newspaper advertisements asking for families to take in these New York children. Those looking for help needed a recommendation from their pastor and a judge. Putting his trust and faith in the benevolence of Protestant strangers, he made it his mission to send the children to *kind Christian homes in the country.* Affiliated ministers in charge of orphanages in various places cared for the children temporarily and helped to find local rural families.

Charles instructed Christian volunteers to help him manage the train logistics, obtain permission from government officials, and convince the families to let their children leave, ultimately resolving the city's problems of poverty and overpopulation. The streets of New York were full of children belonging to (mostly) Catholic immigrants from Ireland, Germany, and Italy as thousands of Europeans poured into the Eastern Harbor on ships. On the crowded streets, their children fetched and fended for themselves and also brought back scraps for their immigrant families, which sometimes included sick parents, siblings or elders. Catholic immigrants were considered to be of inferior stock compared to the Midwesterners who were Protestants and, therefore, assumed to be *good-hearted* people.

Reverend Brace believed that these "little ones of Christ" needed "good influences and kind people." He felt compelled to help the vagrant children who were often stigmatized as *Arabs, drunkards,* or *prostitutes.* The elimination of these particular children from the city assisted rural Midwestern Christian farmers to tend to their land and, at the same time, clean up the streets of the metropolis. At first, the train seemed like an adventure, but once the children realized they would be separated from their siblings and their families, their moods changed to anger and resentment. Some were told where they were headed, and others had no idea, but their status as minors prevented them from contesting the arrangements.

The staff handed out clean dress clothes, a *Bible,* and placed the children on a train headed west equipped with indentured servant papers outlining the terms and conditions of their placement depending on the child's age. Brace expected boys fifteen and older to work until the age of eighteen in exchange for boarding and clothes. He intended for the younger boys to attend school for part of each year and remain until the age of eighteen. Brace instructed the applicants (meaning, the farmers) to treat the boys as "one of their own children in the matters of schooling, clothing, and training."

The trains stopped at rural churches along the way, where eager congregational members gathered and bid on the children who stood on a stage. If a child was not chosen at one location, the staff told them to board the train again for potential takers at the next stop. Reverend Brace hoped that his orphans wrote to him twice a year to keep him informed of their status. Furthermore, he allowed them to keep their true identities intact; they also had the option to leave the farmstead, and the Child Aid Society reserved the right to take the children back. In addition, the staff attempted to match children with people who spoke the same language. One German train rider had to board several times before he was taken in by a German family.

Reverend Brace expected to hear from every child twice a year. A number of the orphans wrote to him, and he organized and preserved these rare letters in a filing system. Based on the letters mailed back to the pastor, the children reported being afraid during their journeys and saddened by the loss of their families. Many admitted to having a hard time transitioning from the city to the country. As adults, many felt angered and resentful after being assigned to live with strangers. However, the problem for these children was that their new parents threatened them into writing only good things about their placements. The intimidations created a quandary for the isolated young recipients. Should they claim that they were happy despite the abuses, or should they paint an accurate picture and risk punishment? A few of the children expressed a fear of being returned to the city after many of the farmers threatened to send them back. After adapting to their new homes, the fear of the unknown kept the youngsters dependent upon the adopters, even the abusive ones.

For the next 37 years (until Charles Loring Brace's death at the age of 64 in 1890), the pastor worked on his Emigration Plan, a welfare program known today as *The Orphan Train Movement,* which is considered the largest forced migration of children in the United States (and the foundation for what we now know as domestic adoptions).

> *Reverend Brace is remembered in many historical accounts as a good man who saved destitute orphans.*

There was no mention of orphan trains during his lifetime, as roughly half of the children came from families. Researcher Stephen O'Conner, author of *Orphan Trains: The Story of Charles Loring Brace and the Children He Saved and Failed,* noted in the prologue that Brace's efforts were referred to as the Home-Finding Department and eventually came to be known as Foster Care. The practice was called *Family Placement* or *Out-Placement.* It was not until after CBS presented a miniseries on the subject that marked the beginning of the reference to *The Orphan Train Movement* after 1978. Another component mentioned by Mr. O'Conner was that "virtually every program seeking to help homeless and needy children was either inspired by or a response to Brace's work and ideas."

Between 1854 and 1929, various accounts estimate that 250,000 children from New York had been transported westward to families of strangers that could be helped by these so-called *unwanted children.* Others put this figure closer to 500,000. Of these numbers, Brace's Protestant organization placed roughly 105,000 children into homes in rural America (although some were sent to Canada or to Indian Territories). Over the entire seventy-five years of this rare epoch in United States history, Reverend Brace's method was believed to be much more humane (and cheaper) than even the best institutional care.

Some of the orphan train descendants try to keep the memory of the movement alive through the upkeep of museums and websites. A staff member from The National Orphan Train Complex, a small museum located in Concordia, Kansas, believes that only about thirty riders are alive today.

Further exploration of Reverend Brace's mission uncovered another perspective, namely accounts from various sources about how mothers were duped into letting their children board the trains after having been given a false impression that they would see their children again. Various immigrant women remained home to care for sick loved ones while they sent their children out to play or to fetch food or other necessities. The children needed (or wanted) the freedom to roam the streets (and to go home at will) in order to help with the care of the household. The eradication of these children might have appeared to be a solution for the minister and his male associates who benefitted from the scheme, but at the same time, their absence created a devastating and damaging role in the lives of the mostly destitute European immigrant families who depended upon them to provide assistance. Critics of the movement point out that the minister and his staff never considered this natural cycle of familial support.[31] While the public ignored the cries and concerns of the separated families, the facilitators flourished.

Mail-Order Kids

"As we call out your number," Sister Ursula said, "please step forward to claim your child. Examine the child we selected for you. If it's satisfactory, take it to your home and treat it as you would your own flesh and blood."

From *Mail Order Kid* by Marilyn Coffer pg. 19

The American children loaded onto trains as early as 1854 were not necessarily *unwanted*, despite some historical accounts that refer to them as *waifs* or *foundlings*, but came from families. The children were led to believe that they were orphaned and labeled as such on documents (which then denied them access to birth certificates and other related documents and assistance for locating, identifying, and reuniting with relatives years later). Just one example of this is a woman by the name of Teresa Martin, who, at age 73, returned to the hospital where she was born in 1906. The nuns turned her away with a terse response: "Your case is closed."

In the PBS documentary, *Orphan Trains*, produced and directed by Janet Graham and Edward Gray, readings from the writings and letters of now-deceased children can be heard transforming stories from the past into vivid narratives. Personal accounts reveal the fear, turmoil, and loss they experienced as children making the forced trek from New York City into unknown areas out West.

Lorraine Williams remembered the details (even though she was only four at the time): "The big day came, and we arrived on a Sunday in Kirksville, Missouri, at the Presbyterian church. We marched down the aisle, thirteen of us, and they would walk past us and you were viewed. And that's a strange feeling. You'd never been looked at in that way before. You'd never seen people looking all around you."

Elliott Hoffman Bobo, age eight, felt insecure at the public viewings and articulated what many others sensed: "I wasn't very comfortable up on that stage because I didn't know where I was going to go. And I was old enough to realize that there could be a lot of mistakes."

Lee Nailing, also eight, mentioned how he intentionally placed a pink envelope given to him by his father into his coat pocket that contained his address. His father told him to be sure to let him know when he and his brothers got to their destination. The next morning, Lee immediately reached into his pocket, but the envelope was gone. "I was kind of heartbroken, of course." He asked for help, but "one of the caretakers came by and asked us what we were doing and [we] told her that we were looking for the envelope. I was afraid to tell her anything else because punishment sometimes was a little severe. And she told me to get up, get in my seat, [because] where I was going I would not need that envelope."

By the time Lee reached a small town in Texas, he had reported that there were about twenty-five children left, including his two-year-old brother. He watched as a couple took him away. "There again, I -- I felt terrible because I knew I was losing a brother right there. And they took Gerald over to the table, did the paperwork, and he was just happy as he could be until they started out the door, and he suddenly realized that he was losing his brothers. And he turned around and screamed right loud for his 'bruvvers.' And, of course, that broke my heart again."

Someone chose Lee and, as a consequence, "After two or

three years, going back to New York was just past thinking." Lee eventually became acclimated to his situation and even reported being happy. However, he said, "My adoptive mother, Mrs. Nailling, lived with a horror that I would eventually go back to New York to my biological people." He further explained, "I don't imagine I would have gone back if I'd have had the chance, but even after I was grown, she had that horror."

Regarding the arrival into her new *loving family,* Claretta Miller, age nine, said, "I knew that this was going to be my home from then on, but it seemed like it just kind of hit me when I got here that I had left everything behind, which I had. I didn't have my sister anymore. I didn't have my parents anymore. I didn't have any friends. They were total strangers. It just caught up with me all at once. But [the woman who chose her] was with me, Mrs. Carmen. She never left me for a minute. And she helped me get into bed, and that's when I began to cry. [...] was when the emotion hit me, I think, when I went to get into bed. I still felt all alone, and yet I knew there was someone around me, but they were strangers. I didn't know them from Adam."

Like many children from similarly-large migrations even today, Alice Ayler was aware of her lower status in relation to the other children in her new adoptive surroundings, "Bad blood. That's what they used to consider it. We kids from New York were of inferior stock."

However, she spoke of being able to become a good mother because of the westward move: "I got to do what I was capable of doing, making something of myself, being a good mother." Of her traumatic beginnings, she said, "It hurt awfully bad, being separated from my family."

Justifying the practice, and affirming that it needs to continue, are common refrains from those who have been adopted. It is something a great many feel obligated to do, becoming almost a habit meant to gain approval after sharing their not-so-*positive* experiences. A happy ending tends to leave the impression that all is well that ends well. Yet, the happy ending had more to do with the adopted person's own will and tenacity to survive, despite being adopted, rather than to the adoption itself.

Marilyn June Coffey, author of *Mail-Order Kid: An Orphan Train Rider's Story*, gave a detailed depiction of the entire landscape during that time, as well as an account of a four-year-old girl sent to Kansas from New York. Coffey mentions that fifty or so orphan-train riders shed tears as they described their childhoods during a reunion decades later.

A rivalry for children erupted between the Protestant and Catholic denominations (from a competing orphanage started by Sister Irene versus the founder of Children's Aid Society (CAS), Charles Loring Brace). When it came to placing children for adoption, religious affiliation was a significant factor: "Brace's Protestant Group, The CAS, soon made Catholic enemies."[32] Coffey briefly hinted at an internal competition between Brace and the Catholic co-founders of Foundlings Hospital. "They [Catholic sisters] hated the way Brace 'snatched' children off the streets and sent them out of the city. They accused him of putting Catholic children into Protestant homes in order to convert them." Furthermore, "because of the jealousy," the staff at New York Foundling Hospital sent Jewish and Protestant babies and toddlers out to the rural Catholic homes. The nuns copied some of Brace's techniques to assist with what was at first called "Baby Trains," then later referred to as "Mercy Trains" by relying on local priests to send about 30,000 children out into the fields.[33]

Coffey mentioned that the orphan train riders suffered "Physical, intellectual, and emotional wounds" and "....a displacement much like an 'exhaustion from a prolonged trauma.'" Some children relayed tales of being treated well or petted and pampered (in the author's words), while others were subjected to abuse. Whether they were foster or adoptive guardians, most of the adult strangers involved were not motivated to treat the children well (because they believed that they were already doing the children a favor by allowing them into their homes in the first place).

A number of the children even needed to learn a new language when they were moved across the country, as was the case with Teresa Martin, the protagonist of *Mail-Order Kid*, a child presented as an orphan and sent to Hays, Kansas, by the Catholic sisters. Hays was a "rough and tough town in its early years of 1867, at one time sporting 37 liquor establishments." A group of Russian Volga Germans (initially named after the longest river in Russia) initially settled in the area to farm.

Little Teresa, whose mother was Jewish, did not know where she was going until she reached her destination. Once there, ministers announced the news to the waiting couples and farmers: "'As we call out your number,' Sister Ursula said, 'Please step forward to claim your child. Examine the child we selected for you. If it's satisfactory, take it to your home and treat it as you would your own flesh and blood.'"[34]

Teresa was one of those children. An elderly German couple with grown children took her by the hand, but they were interrupted by other interested adults:

"Pardon me [...] I'm wondering if I could buy this little girl from you?"

"You wish to buy this child?" the nun asked, but rejected the request because the man was Presbyterian and not Catholic. "I'm afraid it's out of the question. If you were Catholic, we would perhaps consider it."

Teresa remembered the Presbyterian couple offering to take her for cash, but the Catholic man refused to accept because of his Protestant affiliation. The Catholic mother Teresa had been assigned to even arrogantly "switched her long skirt away" and hissed "Jude" as they walked away with Teresa in tow, who did not understand the insult.

At such a young age, Teresa watched these exchanges while the adults selected the other children. She trembled while thinking, "I won't see my mother and father but strangers pretending to be my parents. Why are the Sisters doing this?"[35]

Adoptive Home:

Once arriving at the isolated house on the outskirts of Schoenchen (founded in 1877 and known as the German Capital of Kansas), Teresa was made to sit on the lap of her new *father* while he drank a beer (as if she were already his child). Her new *mother* slapped her face that first night before bed because the four-year-old girl had not yet learned any German. At the orphanage, the nuns routinely gave her a nightgown to wear before bed, but the adoptive parents made little Teresa sleep in her undergarments at this rural homestead.

Did the Catholic nuns know that this new family did not like Jews? The new school environment was also frightening for Teresa. The children called her "a Jew" immediately causing her to feel like an outcast during those formative years.

> *"So you're happy here." Mrs. Spallen made the sound like a statement, not a question.*
>
> *If I say yes, nothing bad will happen, but if I say no, what will she do? Maybe tell Mrs. Bieker, who will slap me later.*
>
> *"Yes."*
>
> *"Good.* [86]

~ Teresa Biecker, adopted in 1910
From Mail-Order Kid

As an adult, this adoptee speculated that she was intentionally sent to a German Catholic family by the Foundling Hospital sisters. *Did her Jewish parents try to find her?* Teresa remembered reading that "Catholic orphanages refused to return Jewish children to their parents." This triggered curiosity.

Eventually, Teresa wondered if she could get more answers if she traveled to the hospital. When she got there, it dawned on her that she was not the only orphan-train rider. She quietly accepted her life situation, but when a nun disclosed that they had placed

5,000 New York children into Kansas homes, Teresa no longer felt so isolated! She was not the only one!

As a senior citizen, she did attempt to politely retrieve her birth certificate, but she overhead a nun say, "Thank God, someone came back who was cheerful and didn't complain." Teresa thought to herself:

'I could complain, too! My Schoenchen home wasn't the greatest.

However, she said nothing aloud.[37] Upon Teresa's death, she remained loyal to the Catholic Church and to the nuns despite never reuniting with her Jewish mother (nor was she given answers after inquiring about her). In the 1960s, and at the age of 73, she was told face-to-face: "Your case is closed." She had already heard this answer twice before. This was her last attempt.

Even as a toddler of four years, Teresa Bieker, adopted in 1910, opposed the idea of being given a new name. A priest tried to console her, claiming how *lucky* she was because not all her friends "got to be somebody's child." Meanwhile, she wondered, *How will her mother find her if everyone called her by a different name?*

Back to the Future:

On June 15, 2014, The *New York Times* published an article, "New York Adoptees Fight for Access to Birth Certificates," echoing a complaint heard on forums from the Internet about antiquated adoption laws that date back to the 1930s. More and more of today's adopted people are compelled to unearth their ancestry for medical reasons but, as one woman stated in the article, "My original birth certificate sits in a building in New York City, and I'm not entitled to it."[38]

When Demand Turns from Boys to Girls

How did America grow to love adoption? Additional answers can be found in the book, *The Baby Thief: The Untold Story of Georgia Tann, the Baby Seller Who Corrupted Adoption*, by Barbara Bisantz Raymond.

> *"[Tann] commercialized adoption. Moreover, the other thing is, she was the first to issue false birth certificates for adopted children, a practice that became standard throughout the United States,"* Ms. Raymond told The Commercial Appeal in 2007.39

Georgia Tann, born to an influential family on July 18, 1891, spearheaded what is known today as *domestic adoption*. During her childhood and into adulthood, she tried to win the approval of her father, a prominent judge in the Mississippi Second Chancery District Court, referred to as having an emotionally cold demeanor, with a reputation for being arrogant, argumentative and domineering. Moreover, a former neighbor declared, "a womanizer." The judge became known for *finding homes for orphans,* but Georgia heard him complain that he wished he could enlist the help of others, such as a judge, teacher, and minister.

"[Judge George Tann] was the most influential person in her life. Her feelings toward him were a mix of love and hate, or wanting to prove herself to him and to defy him."[40]

While Judge Tann was known for his iron will, his daughter "possessed a strong personality and drive." She had a reputation for being selfish, narcissistic, and it was thought that she lacked empathy. The father/daughter relationship caused critics of the practice to suspect that her charity work had been motivated by her need for parental and authoritative approval. By forming a successful child protection and welfare network, Georgia could win positive attention from her stern father.

Georgia's brother, the son of Judge and Mrs. Tann, was adopted, alleges Georgia's second cousin, but the author of *The Baby Thief* could not verify that claim since the state's adoption records remained sealed. The boy was three years older than Georgia, yet it was Georgia who had been named after their father, George.[41] Since firstborns are typically named after fathers, it is easy to suspect that Georgia's older brother was, more than likely, adopted privately.

Between the years of 1924 and 1950, Georgia, acted as a social worker, operating Tann's Tennessee Children's Home Society (a baby farm). She was so influential and so well respected by the community that she even counseled Eleanor Roosevelt on the issue of child welfare, and was personally invited to Truman's Presidential Inauguration, and collaborated with Pearl Buck on adoptions (which led to intercountry adoptions from China through Welcome House, an organization Ms. Buck co-founded with three others in 1949).[42] In Ms. Buck's view, *not* adopting Chinese children was considered racist. Despite Tann's charitable reputation in public, those who worked closely with her, most notably a social worker from the Children's Bureau,[43] described her as ruthless. Much like her father, Georgia was haughty and boastful.

Ms. Tann laid the groundwork for domestic adoption through an expansive network of professionals, consisting of social workers, doctors, nurses, politicians, legislators, attorneys, and another judge (by the name of Camille Kelley) that were used to manage the necessary bribery and corruption involved. Armed with the intent to obtain the rights of children by court order, the judge routinely visited the orphanage run by the Sisters of the Good Shepherd, jotted notes on potentially adoptable children, and ultimately sent them to Ms. Tann. Whenever word got out that Judge Kelley was coming, "[an orphanage employee] and the other sisters would scramble around, trying to hide the prettiest children from her."

Judge Kelley awarded Ms. Tann legal guardianship of the children (a method much like the Holts would use later in South Korea), and then Tann gave her a cut of the profits collected for the children's placements. Within the State of Tennessee, Ms. Tann received only seven dollars. For an adoption placement outside of the state, she received a $5,000 commission. Today *placements* of foreign-born children bring the highest profits.

> *Placements are also called matching or providing a service. This kind of glossy verbiage, according to some equal rights proponents and adoptee activists, prevents facilitators from being accused of child trafficking.*

As early as 1929, Georgia easily attracted potential clients from running newspaper advertisements. The announcements included a photo of a small, well-dressed child with the caption: "Madge is five years old and 'awful lonesome.'" In a little more than a year, Ms. Tann ran approximately 400 of these want-ads, and soon she received so many applications from prospective clients that her two-suite office filled up. "She had also crafted a technique that survives to this day: the advertisement of children for the purpose of sale."[44] Her work made adoption a "household word in the region. By 1935, she had sent American children to all forty-eight states," as well to Mexico, and to Canada, and as far as Panama and England.[45]

Ms. Tann harvested babies from young, unwed, inexperienced, and otherwise disadvantaged mothers. "She considered herself to be above the law, free to make her own rules."[46] The susceptible mothers, influenced by her air of authority, relinquished the rights to their offspring, typically without much trouble.

To find potential at-risk mothers, she published ads like this: "Young women in trouble, call Miss Georgia Tann." She and her employees frequently visited doctors in Tennessee and surrounding states, offering unwed mothers "free room, board, and medical care for the duration of the[ir] pregnancies."

Trained social workers blatantly knocked on doors and told unwed mothers about the children's home, giving the impression that relinquishing parental responsibilities worked out to be in the child's best interest. In addition, Ms. Tann networked with hospital staff. The doctors and nurses, aware of unwed mothers who had just given birth, gave her leads. They might tell the women that their babies were disabled, sick, or needed hospital care and then made them sign papers while they were still drugged. Sometimes staff members claimed that the babies were stillborn.[47] Tann avoided conflict by recording the adopters as the *legal parents* on the newborn's birth certificate. This strategy legitimized her work. The baby's parents could then be documented as having abandoned the child.

Later, after signing away their rights, the exploited parents might approach the children's home only to learn that their children had already been sent to another state and into the welcoming arms of a well-to-do family. Today, the same tactic is used, but *help* is offered via websites that give support and answers for *unplanned* or *crisis* pregnancies. The same verbiage and incentives are used to convince scared pregnant women leading them to believe that they would make inadequate parents.

Whereas the Orphan Train Movement
targeted older and stronger boys capable
of working on farms, it was Tann who,

after the movement ended in 1929, shifted the focus to a more privileged and elite clientele. Tann profited from the wealthy and famous.

Well-to-do folks, eager to adopt girls, paid as much as $10,000, "equivalent to $140,000 today."[48] Her favorite clients were the wealthy from New York and Los Angeles, with her list including Hollywood stars like Joan Crawford, June Allyson, Dick Powell, and Lana Turner. "Georgia's clients sought *babies*, the younger, the better."

After Tann died of cancer in September of 1950, a Tennessee governor finally made public the results of an investigation that uncovered "a vast illegal black market child adoption ring." However, nothing was done for the families who had lost their children. Ms. Tann had enjoyed as much as eighty-to-ninety percent of the money received for her out-of-state placements. Worse, so many of the tiny inmates in her Children's Home had died of malnutrition and neglect that the county she worked in had the highest infant mortality rate in the United States at the time.

For adoptees who were placed during that era, and have questions regarding the ethics of their placements, it is impossible to acquire the information necessary to find their families. "[Tann] went to great pains to erase the identities of the children she took," one journalist reported. "The birth certificates, biographies, and histories of the adopted children were falsified."

Well-to-do adoptive parents feared the risk of being forced to return children if an investigation occurred. Most lived in denial and dismissed the problem.

What happened to the mothers of these babies? Most spent their entire lives blaming themselves for *abandoning* their infants. Not knowing that they had been targeted because of their financial difficulties, they suffered from shame, guilt, and sorrow. These emotions last a lifetime.

As evidenced by *The Baby Thief*, the dangers of intentionally presenting children to the mainstream as *orphans* were obvious. As if they were production units to be sold off of an assembly line, Georgia Tann made it her mission to *rescue* "every single *orphan*." During her dubious career, she managed to change the fate of more than five-thousand babies and was, ultimately, celebrated as a hero for placing them into her *better homes* throughout her professional life. Many of the babies died; however, from the immediate confiscation from their mothers (at times, this was only hours after being born). "[Tann] was trying to place every child in Memphis. She wanted to get her hands on every single child she could."[49]

For today's overseas adoptee, the fanatical desire to "save every single child" sounds eerily familiar to Georgia's efforts. Ms. Tann transformed a formerly glorified practice, built primarily by religious organizations, to a more-glamorized and *legalized* place in mainstream American society.[50]

"Adoption was built on the current foundation of crimes and lies and obvious coercion, but that kinder [...] gentler face of adoption was just remarketed, slicker, but just as coercive[,] if not more subtle and more deadly[,] because they had perfected the seduction."

Claudia Corrigan D'Arcy,
From the website Musings of the Lame[51]

American Herstory

The Toll of Adoption on Mothers

> *"We're getting older, and we're terrified we're going to die ...without getting some acknowledgment that a crime was committed against us ... six million of us. [...] The industry's biggest fear is that someone's going to listen to us. We don't want this to happen to another generation."*

Sandy Young of the Baby Scoop Era From *The Child Catchers: Rescue, Trafficking, and the New Gospel of Adoption*, by Kathryn Joyce[52]

The Baby-Scoop Era, from the end of World War II through the early 1970s, affected at least four million mothers.[53] It is increasingly harder for agencies to continue to pretend that these women do not exist. The practice of sealing previously-public adoption records and, instead, issuing amended birth certificates had begun, and *young unwed* mothers became the most natural target. Agencies could routinely speak for the women (as if they represented them). Meanwhile, these women were expected to remain in the background, told that they should be ashamed and grateful to receive such generous *assistance* so that they could go on to live *successful,* unburdened lives.

"The general public assumption seems to be that, from the beginning, adoption records were closed in large part to protect the birth mother's identity. But that isn't the case at all."[54]

The public was led to believe that the concealment was to protect the identities of all parties involved. However, based on observations of the industry today, a growing number of exploited mothers suspect that the falsifying of information had more to do with thwarting *fallen* women from locating their children. Socialite Georgia Tann, a social worker and agency owner, was a prime example of this phenomenon. "As Georgia increasingly augmented her supply of orphans with kidnapped children, she falsified their ages to prevent their birth parents from finding them."[55]

On the surface, adoption procedures seemed justified and, therefore, were rapidly expanded, state-by-state. Pregnant women of certain social standings were cast-off to homes for unwed mothers under clouds of shame, and their children were stigmatized as *illegitimate,* painting a dogmatic humiliation onto these young mothers. Few had the audacity to discuss their secretive circumstances. Respect for client privacy provided a justification for facilitators to prevent mothers from learning the location of their children (and vice versa). Most industry insiders spent more time with adopters, and as a consequence, it was easier to place blame on the inexperienced and isolated mothers. As a result, the industry catered to their client's wishes and needs (since they were the ones who had paid the fees). *The Washington Post* pointed this out in "How Adoption in America Grew Secret - Birth Records Were not Closed for the Reasons You Might Think," by Professor Elizabeth Samuel. Various US states closed records "to protect adoptive families." Her research further found that "they did so not to provide lifelong anonymity for birth mothers, but the other way around -- to protect adoptive families from possible interference or harassment by birth parents." [56]

The people who obtained children from Georgia Tann particularly didn't want to have their cases investigated. The prevailing midcentury attitude was to leave the topic well enough alone. (That way, there were no problems.) Blaming *birth* parents evolved into the primary tactic used by adoption facilitators to rationalize their actions. Valerie Andrews, Executive Director of Origins Canada, has also addressed this issue and written an article called, "The Language of Adoption." The industry coined the term *birthmothers* to reduce the value and self-esteem of young, inexperienced mothers to merely *birthers* who *gifted their children* to *better families*. Later, these young parents were blamed for the barriers to open records. They were supposed to live with the shame and embarrassment of relinquishment, despite the fact that it was presented to her at the time as an *opportunity*.[57]

Included in America's Baby Scoop Era are the current and collective voices of *Exiled Mothers*, a group of women who have lost children to adoption, *not by informed choice*, but through *fraud, coercion,* and *force*. *Exiled Mothers* state in "Adoption Facts: Why Adoption Records are Closed" that "Our babies were NOT *gifts*. They were NOT *unwanted*." The blog's mission is to "present the truth about adoption." The website goes on to explain that mothers have been "silenced for decades by shame and guilt." And they have suffered alone, believing that they were the only ones. Social workers told them coldly to "forget" to *put the past behind them* and to *get over it*. Truthfully, these mothers never stopped loving their offspring.

Reform activists are calling for interested persons to "sign the petition to open adoptee records," revealing the truth that "no birth parent confidentiality or privacy was promised or desired," in an effort to be heard over the pro-adoption rhetoric and to put the brakes on the "machine."

Throughout the history of adoption, evidence has mounted that it has been paying the clients most terrified of open records. Books written by adopters, like *How to Adopt a Child* (1956), by Ernest and Frances Cady, claimed that: "No good is ever accomplished, and much heartbreak and disillusion for everyone [is] caused by leaving open any avenue by which a natural parent can reappear, uninvited and unwanted..." Adopters have historically expressed that their greatest fear is a potential reunion between *their* [adopted] child(ren) and the biological parents.

By the 1960s, the natural interest to know one's identity sprouted within the adoptee consciousness, and small groups began to engage in informal private discussions. By the 1980s, adoption experts rebranded the practice to include *open* adoption when research illustrated that co-parenting proved better for the children over *closed* adoptions. *Birth* mothers were lured into the practice with the promise that they could maintain contact with their child(ren) at the discretion of the adoptive parents, referred to as the *real parents* so as not to upset the adopted children. There was an attempt to remove the secret shame in an attempt to share parental rights. However, the problem with this reform (or repackaging) became evident in the so-called *progressive* adoptions of today, seen in cases of domestically-adopted individuals and individuals adopted from overseas. For the first year or so, the adoptive parents might send one or two photos. But as soon as the honeymoon phase ends, they often forget (or fail) to comply with their part of the bargain. *Legally,* the adoptive parental authorities hold all rights to do whatever they want. The challenges with these contracts have been that prospective adopters would make promises on applications, but then fail to fulfill them, leaving the exploited parents behind and waiting to receive some sort of correspondence from their child(ren). By this time, the adoption facilitator is out of the picture, no longer in business, or already plundering new territories decades later when the adoptee is old enough to inquire. *Open* adoptions became a prevalent practice in the United States, but fail when adopters move away, refuse to include the child's family, or unintentionally give the impression that the child's mother is somehow inferior to the new strangers in his, or her, life. The adopted are then caught between having to prove their loyalty to two opposing factions.

In 1993, Michelle McColm of Adoption Reunions wrote, "Keeping the records closed protects insecure adoptive parents from competing for the love and loyalty of birth parents.

Throughout the years, social workers have to assure the adoptive parents that the birth mother would never reappear."

It is true that a significant amount of adopters are intimidated by the thought of potential reunions. It has been reported that the "government-sanctioned reunion registries" cause some [adopters] even to feel betrayed.[58]

Another adopter affirms what a good many others secretly hope: "We were told that we would never see [the child's mother] or have contact with her."[59]

As a consequence of all this *protection*, numerous adoptees confide the resistance they receive from both adoptive parents and the adoptive communities. Should adoptees search? Or should they be complacent? This is a lifelong question.

The Risk of Suicide

The *birth* mothers in this study overwhelmingly described their experience of relinquishment as traumatic. Responding to the statement

> *"Relinquishing my child was a traumatic experience, 89% answered that this statement was "Extremely true;" 96% of the respondents answered either "Extremely true" or "Very true." The three positive responses combined ("extremely / very / somewhat true") accounted for 99% of the responses.*[60]

A personal note from the author: My sister and I were privileged to be able to attend a conference coordinated by Origins, Canada, held in Toronto, Canada. The atmosphere at the 2012 conference, organized by mothers in the adoption reform movement, was vastly different from those led by pro-adoption professionals, *experts,* adopters, and even adoptees. At the conference led by mothers, an air of sadness and grief permeated the air. In contrast, the mood at adoption agency and adoptee funded conferences were celebratory and reeked of success. In *adoptive parent* environments, *adoptees* and *families of loss* risk being branded as *negative* or *anti-adoption*, when they express honesty. To be included in the discourse, they must remain mute.

Parents grieve today; their voices seep into the public, and they sometimes speak of suicide on occasion. I came across an online comment by a mother about her reaction to her loss, a voice as-yet-unheard by those who maintain the current system. She admitted: "I remember thinking that as soon as I had my baby and gave her up, I was going to kill myself. That was my plan. I guess some would say that was my so-called *adoption plan*. The one and only thing that has changed AND saved my life is my son. I've never thought about [suicide] since."

Others admit to how grieving can manifest through various ways, like drug abuse, smoking, overeating, or excessive drinking.

> *"In response to items concerning depression, 51% of the respondents reported experiencing severe depression since the relinquishment, with 97% reporting some degree of depression (mild, moderate, or severe). Over half reported experiencing depression often since the relinquishment. 63% have had thoughts about killing themselves.* [161]

The issue of suicide was brought up in the safety of a forum for mothers-of-loss only, revealing that they think constantly about their children and, sometimes, grieve endlessly for them. Mothers say that those who claim that adoption is "very emotional, personal and exhausting, have absolutely NO grasp of what women go through when that baby is taken from them."

A Single Piece of Information

Special Contribution by Lorraine Dusky

Life can change with a single piece of information, as it did for thousands of people when Florence Fisher placed a "want ad" in *The New York Times*: "Adult who was an adopted child desires contact with other adoptees to exchange views on adoptive situation and for mutual assistance in search for natural parents."

Fisher's first attempt to place the notice was rebuffed by someone who said she didn't have a real "organization" and huffily rejected it. The next morning—a Saturday—she called back, got someone else, and asked for help writing the copy. The above ad appeared that Sunday, March 21, 1971.

Hundreds of letters flooded into Fisher's apartment in New York City. A month later, a story about her and what she was up to appeared in *The Daily News*. Before it ran, the writer urged her to get a post office box to handle the mountain of mail she undoubtedly would get. He instinctively understood that his column would unleash a flood of responses. This outside observer knew what legislators today are still denying: Adopted individuals want and need to know their true stories about the beginning of their lives and, conversely, a great many mothers are desperate to know what happened to their children and reconnect.

It was not always this way. Beginning in 1917 in Minnesota

and continuing for the next half-century, all states but two (Alaska and Kansas) enacted laws sealing an individual's original birth certificate after the adoption was finalized, and replacing it with an amended one. The new parents' names were substituted for the biological parents and, in some cases, the place—and even date—of birth were altered.

Fisher was not the first to recognize and to do battle against the social engineering that the sealed-records statutes represent. Another adopted individual, Jean Paton, had already broken that ground in 1954 with *The Adopted Break Silence,* a collection of 40 stories by others writing about their own adoption experiences. In 1968, she told her own story in *Orphan Voyage.* Both books had limited distribution but, by the 1970s, she had a burgeoning correspondence with adoptees and natural mothers, a phrase some still prefer, and the first adoptee/biological mother registry. But while Paton was certainly the first "orphan" to publicly speak up against the erasure of the family of origin on adoptee "birth" certificates, she lived in a small town in Colorado, far from any major media outlets.

It took Florence Fisher, with her fiery temperament and red hair to match, as well as her location in America's media epicenter of New York City, to break through the sound barrier to ignite the nascent adoption reform movement. Her own memoir, *The Search for Anna Fisher,* came out in 1973, but news of it had not reached me.

It took a long feature in *The New York Times* about Fisher on July 25, 1972, to awaken me. The headline says it all: "Adopted Children Who Wonder, 'What Was Mother Like?'"[62] Along with thousands of others, I learned about ALMA, the Adoptees Liberty Movement Association Fisher had founded. Her goal was to: a) unseal original birth certificates and b) allow mothers and their children to reunite.

I can recall the electrifying moment when I read the story in my living room. I had relinquished a child to adoption in 1966, and I was beset with anxiety about her, running like never-off white noise in the background of my life.

*Was she all right? Healthy? Were her
new parents good to her? Did she have
the better life I had envisioned when I, a
single woman, gave her up for adoption?
Could I ever know her? Would she ever
want to know me? Could she ever
understand why I had not kept
her? Would she forgive me?*

Though I knew one other woman who had also relinquished a child (a confession over lunch with a co-worker led to her own revelation), I'd never had a conversation with anyone who was adopted about their feelings. My husband at the time knew, but not his family, and we had no plans to ever tell them. The sense of isolation we women felt was a secret prison that held us without a release date. The sorrow and shame bore a hole right through our hearts and fortified the wall of silence that had been instilled in us by society. In special homes for unwed mothers, as they were called, the girls and young women there were encouraged not to use their real names and never reveal them. To spare the family embarrassment, other teens ended up with relatives far from home. Deep in the closet myself, I had hidden my pregnancy and the birth and adoption of my daughter from my family who lived in another state. So deeply shamed was I when that when I told my editor at the Rochester newspaper where I was working that I would be quitting, I made up a story—my father was sick and my mother needed me at home—rather than admit the truth. It got sticky when he tried to talk me out of quitting, couldn't I just take a leave of absence? I was too ashamed to agree. I went into hiding in my own apartment.

I was merely one of the luckless crowd who became pregnant in the decades after World War II without someone to marry. It is estimated that just over a quarter of all children born in the United States to women between the ages of 15 and 29 in the decade between 1960 and 1970 were conceived outside of marriage. Those who wanted an abortion faced grim hurdles, for it was illegal, scary, difficult to obtain, and often performed under unsafe conditions with anesthesia. If marriage was out of the question, adoption was presented as The Answer. Families were mortified and pressured luckless teenagers to give up their babies. Afterward, we were supposed to keep on walking like nothing had happened, as if a part of us had not been left behind. Only a brave few could find the mental and financial resources to keep their babies. So many children were placed for adoption in the years following World War II up to 1973 that the period is known as the Baby Scoop Era.

Adoption as a topic of conversation was under the radar in those decades. The numbers might have gone up, but no one talked about it except in hushed tones. The media largely ignored it. An untold number of people were never even told that they were adopted, even as everyone else in the family knew. The lucky few whose parents stayed mum sometimes found out from cousins or neighborhood friends. I call them "lucky" because that was better than finding out decades later, at, say, the time of a parent's death when a relative had loose lips, or a squabble over inherited family jewelry erupted. Even today, late-discovery adoptees are still popping up.

Yet that morning *The New York Times* gave me proof that adoption as I was living it was wrong at its very core. It had been wrong when I relinquished my daughter, and I knew it then. When I learned what the law was in New York when I was pregnant, I had protested long and loud to my social worker at the agency. I begged for my daughter to at least have the right to know who I was when she became an adult. She could make her own decision if she wanted to seek me out, what could be wrong with that? But the social worker, though sympathetic, could offer no alternative. I was a voice crying out into the void where no one would listen. The law was the law, she said. It is what it is.

So when Florence Fisher and ALMA
shone a light on what was wrong with
closed, secret adoption, thousands, nay,

> *millions of mothers and their grown-up*
> *children lost to the system saw a way out*
> *of their private hell. Soon I was on my*
> *way to joining a movement that would*
> *reshape the rest of my life.*

Within months after that story appeared, I began writing stories for national publications—*Cosmopolitan, Parents, Newsweek*—about the injustice of closed adoptions, and the promise of the reform movement. The focus was always on the adopted individual. Left out was any more than a slight reference to the devastating psychological effect on the mothers who gave up their children. We were the sinners. We deserved what we got. We were still bound by society's code of silence. No matter, every story resulted in hundreds of letters from bereft individuals, the grown-up adopted "children" and their grieving mothers.

The newly formed National Council for Adoption, or NCFA, and experts from the adoption industry who saw their business changing, bleated out dire warnings. The attitude was: adoptees are supposed to be grateful for being "saved" by adoption, for who knows what awful fate would have awaited them otherwise, and mothers were supposed to disappear and, for god's sake, shut up. It was terrifying to admit, even to good friends or to a fiancé, that you were one of "those women."

As ALMA took up the mission to repeal and replace sealed-records laws, it was soon clear that without the mothers speaking out that they too wanted information about their children and possible reunion, progress would be halted. Legislators had to get past thinking that we mothers had stopped caring about their relinquished children. They needed to know that a great many of us were left with a deep well of unresolved grief that could not heal without answers. Our children might want to know who they were at birth. We wanted to know who they were now. And a great many of us yearned for a reunion.

Yet the retort from legislators was always: What about the women who were "promised" anonymity? (Even though the laws did not actually promise the mothers anything of the sort.) But that was implied with the sealed-records statutes! We don't want to ruin their lives! That adopted child will be a stranger knocking on their door! What if their husbands don't know? Their children? Maybe they have moved on with their lives and don't want to be reminded? What about them?

I felt as if I had no choice: I had to speak out. I divorced the same year that the article in *The New York Times* appeared, so I no longer had to worry about the reaction of my husband or the in-laws. I told my family the whole truth and that I was going to speak out. They supported me.

Writing about a court case in which I had testified for an adoptee who wanted her records from an agency, I admitted my own connection to the case in an op-ed for *The New York Times* in 1975.[63] Writing for *Town & Country* a year later—the rich adopt, don't they?—I was even more forthright and began the piece with these words: "Ten years ago I had a child whom I gave up for adoption."[64] That landed me on *The Today Show*, wondering if my daughter or her parents were watching.

That same year, 1976, the New York State legislature was considering a bill that would unseal the original birth certificates (OBC) to the adopted, which had been sealed since the 1930s. A public hearing was held in Albany. Fisher and adoptee author, Betty Jean Lifton, and I testified. Among the others speaking that day was a representative of New York Foundling Home, a nun who said her agency had found about half of the hundred or so natural mothers who returning adoptees had asked them to find. Surprisingly, no one on the panel asked how many of the mothers had refused to meet their children.

I sought her out during a break and asked her myself. "None," she replied. "Most were delighted to be found. One had been reluctant at first," she said, "and then changed her mind."

After I read my prepared statement, and after I stated what the nun from the Foundling Home had told me, one of the legislators pressed me on the issue of women who might wish to stay unknown, fearing, he said, the "trauma of confrontation."

> *When I said that no mother's right should supersede that of the adoptee, that any supposed right of secrecy granted to the mother infringed on the rights of the adopted, a lawyer for Louise Wise, one of the major New York City agencies, Shad Polier, let out an exasperated sigh heard throughout the chamber. When he spoke, he used words such as "disaster," "harmful," "pathology," and "havoc."[65]*

No legislation passed, that year or the next. Or the next.

Because of the entrenchment of the adoption industry, and the public's beatific opinion of adoptive parents, language was already an issue between the two sides—those involved in search and reunion, and those upholding the old laws. Natural mother, which Florence and I preferred, made adoptive parents, and prospective adoptive parents, uncomfortable. If one mother was "natural," that made them the opposite. To alleviate the antipathy, Lee Campbell, the founder of Concerned United Birthparents (CUB) used the words "birthparent" and "birthmother" when she formed her new organization that same year. The less offensive term to agencies and adoptive parents was readily taken up and ultimately became the standard. However, today the term has become highly controversial among in the adoption reform movement.*

But that is now. The hostility toward women who relinquished children and had the nerve to speak up and against sealed records was intense and pervasive. In the year before she formed CUB, Campbell herself stayed veiled when she appeared on television, and anonymous when interviewed for newspaper stories. Her appearances were controversial and elicited both empathy and antagonism from the audience.

The next year, 1977, Fisher, under the umbrella of ALMA, instituted a class-action lawsuit in federal court against New York's sealed adoption records law, which dated from the 1930s.

"Apart from slavery there is no other instance in our laws, or in any other jurisprudence in civilized system of jurisprudence, in which a contract made among adults, in respect of an infant, can bind that child once he reaches his majority," wrote attorney Cyril Means in his brief for ALMA. The fullness of the meaning in those words has encouraged me when we encountered a setback. How could not everyone grasp their absolute rightness? We in the movement stayed hopeful, believing that one day adoptees everywhere would have the right to know their original, accurate, full history and ancestry.

Antagonism toward mothers who relinquished was still rampant in 1979 when I published my memoir, *Birthmark*, the first to present a natural mother's perspective.[66] Numerous publishers rejected the work because of the topic before I found a publisher. My understanding and supportive agent spared me much of what she heard, but I learned enough to know that many female editors she approached were squeamish about publishing a memoir with a storyline they deemed trashy, and by extension, the writer. Nearly all the female editors of that era were from America's upper class, women who graduated from select private schools and who grew up with the dictum that their names should appear in a newspaper three times: at birth, marriage, and death. With my blue-collar Polish background, I was not one of them, and I had written what they deemed a tawdry story to boot. That I had gotten pregnant outside of marriage was bad enough, but to be public about it? Write a memoir? *Horrors!* Besides, they had friends who had adopted, or they might want to adopt themselves one day, and who wanted to deal with *that woman*?

On the other side of the spectrum was the reaction of a male publisher's right-hand man. The publisher was known for taking on gutsy works; we met at a Manhattan literary saloon. He had brought along his right-hand man, who hadn't known the subject of my memoir. As soon as he grasped it, his face turned red with rage, and he began ranting at me. I can still recall his fury, instant and unabated. I quickly excused myself and went to the ladies' room, now quite shaken myself. When I returned, the third man was gone. The publisher told me that his friend and employee had grown up in an orphanage and had no idea who his mother was, facts about the man's life that he never knew before. Of course, he was sorry, but he couldn't consider my book now.

The thirteenth submission found an enthusiastic editor/publisher, a man with a background nothing like mine, or the elite literary types who had turned the memoir down flat. Some talk shows refused to interview me because the host "is an adoptive parent," show bookers stated matter-of-factly to my publisher's publicist. End of story. News programs sometimes sent reporters who would rather have had my head than let me find my daughter. I would be pilloried with suspicion and anger in one interview, only to find acceptance and compassion in the next. Several newspapers had adoptive parents review *Birthmark*, revealing more about the author's anxieties rather than the memoir itself. Thus the book itself was not reviewed, but the issue of openness was on trial, and the verdict was often negative.

Coincidentally, the year *Birthmark* came out is the same year the ALMA's lawsuit was dismissed on merits and lost on appeal. The decision reaffirmed what we heard in legislator's offices when we lobbied: Adoptee rights had to be balanced with birth parent privacy, as well as "the family unit already in existence."[67] Our disappointment was keen, but nobody gave up the fight. We knew right was on our side. The American Adoption Congress, comprised of birth mothers, adoptees, and adoptive parents, held its first conference that year in Washington, DC. The AAC would become a champion of unsealing adoption records.

Yet that same year, 28 states defeated or allowed bills to die in committee that would have given adult adoptees some access to information in sealed records.[68] Despite the setbacks, some heard our plight. A federal department of Health, Education, and Welfare (HEW) was working on a model adoption act to unify the myriad state laws regarding adoption, and it was holding hearings around the country to gather input from experts as well as the public. The adoption reform movement, now known as ARM, was making headway. We were thrilled that Lee Campbell was on the committee that would write the bill. Lifton, Fisher, and I spoke at the hearing in New York City—along with adoptive parents, social workers, adoption agency heads, adoption attorneys, judges. The mood was shifting in the country, but those against us were vehement in their opposition. Their fury could shatter glass when they spoke.

Yet when HEW released its proposed model adoption act, it contained these words:

> *"Secrecy is not and has never been an essential or substantive aspect of adoption."*

We won! I thought. Everyone wanted to celebrate! The report went on: "There can be no legally protected interest in keeping one's identity secret from one's biological offspring: Parents and child are considered co-owners of the information regarding the event of birth…the birth parents' interest in reputation is not alone deserving of constitutional protection." Surely this was the blow that would knock out sealed records.

Later, Florence—we became lifelong friends—and I would troop up to Washington DC for a hearing on this part of the act, both of us making strong statements for passage. The head of the committee, adoptive father and well-known drunk in Washington, the late Senator John Tower of Texas, did not even bother to attend. The language that would unseal birth records was deleted from the final act.

We licked our wounds but did not give up. This was a setback, not the end.

While progress was stymied on the legal front, people were moving forward in the underground, just as slaves and abolitionists had operated before the found before the 13th amendment freed them. Mothers and adoptees were being reunited. How it was done was passed on to others, *sotto voce*, for it was illegal, one supposes, but it was happening. Understanding social workers at agencies sometimes gave up desired names, or left the room with the open adoption file on the desk—do what you will—or contacted mothers themselves, some of whom had left letters and their forwarding addresses at the agencies. Stories circulated about certain clerks in certain locations who, for a small fee, copied the original birth certificate and surreptitiously passed it on in the women's room. I wrote my agency in Rochester three times but got nowhere.

But I had heard of a mysterious searcher who found children for mothers, and mothers for children, seemingly with ease. Reaching him or her was through an underground network, and strictly cash only. I paid $1,200 to someone who knew someone who knew someone—it really was that convoluted—to find my daughter in 1981. Nine years after I first learned of Florence Fisher and ALMA, I was reunited with my 15-year-old daughter in the Madison, Wisconsin airport with her adoptive father looking on. The person who had passed on her name— again through a third party—I later learned, had already located her through the clues I had written into *Birthmark*. I had hoped that her parents would read it and reach out to me. Her adoptive mother, an avid reader, had been told about the book by a relative, she related to me later but had not read it. But she and her husband had already tried to locate me due to our daughter's epilepsy, and, much to my immense relief, they welcomed me into their lives.

By the mid-80s, indeed, talk show after talk show, including some of the very same that wouldn't touch the subject five years earlier, now found that it generated high ratings. One of the very shows that had turned me down, with the same host, now wanted me, and I turned her down. My daughter and I were on one local show in Boston. The New York Times did a big story featuring me and another reunited mother and daughter.[69] Producers brought mothers and their adult children together on live television, which some in the movement found objectionable, but that did pay for the transportation if the two were hundreds of miles apart. Florence, telling the adoptee's story, was especially popular and effective on television, and the public lapped it up. Some thought the shows exploitive, but such publicity always focused on the issue of sealed birth certificates and the intense longing for the parties to reconnect. I debated Elizabeth Bartholet, a furious but articulate Harvard Law professor and adoptive mother, on a popular PBS show. She was propped up by a phalanx of adoption attorneys via a feed from elsewhere, and all opposed to me. She called all of the research showing that being adopted was traumatic to the individual, "garbage." That is a direct quote.

But no matter the venue or the tenor of the encounter, all media on the issue brought more adoptees and mothers out of the woodwork, as well as frantic and nasty pushback from adoptive parents and dire warnings about the future of the adoption industry and adoption attorneys. Yes, there was increasing acceptance, but we were still on the outside. Adoptees were painted as disgruntled and angry. Mothers who spoke out were seen as outliers, not as representatives of the many. Yet we persisted. Nothing could stop the forward momentum of adoptee rights. Even NCFA's outspoken founder, William Pierce, who publicly opposed us at every turn, admitted privately to Fisher that one day the sealed records would be open.

As the decades ticked by, I continued to write pieces about unsealing OBCs for magazines and newspapers around the country wherever there was an active push for unseal legislation. Alabama closed their open records in the middle of all this activity, only to reopen them a decade later. Sandy Musser, who found her adopted daughter, and helped many others do the same, was caught by a sting operation, and ended up in jail.

Yet slowly but surely, some states began to unseal their previously sealed records, starting with Oregon in 1998 after a voter referendum. The general public appears to grasp the issue better than legislators. Oregon's law was challenged in court but defeated.

DNA connections in the last couple of decades have certainly pushed the needle toward connection, as many families—siblings and parents and children—are connected that way. But that is the side door. *Open adoptions*, in which the parties know each other before the adoption, is a better alternative than *closed* or *anonymous adoptions*, but both sets of parents in these arrangements sometimes find it difficult to stay connected or do not even try. One disappointed first mother—a term slowly evolving into our language—showed me the promised photo of her child she was sent; the picture shows the back of the head of her baby. Not all adoptive parents are this way, but enough are to make open adoption agreements iffy. Laws governing maintaining the connection invariably come down in favor of the parent with the child, that is, the adoptive parent.

Only after more decades of exhaustive lobbying, hearings, and op-eds and essays on the subject, did New York in 2020 unseal without restriction to adoptees their original birth certificates. Nearly half a century had passed since that first hearing on the issue in the state capitol. In the time between 1976 and 2020, nine other states, all smaller in population than New York, unsealed their records to adoptees without restrictions; but more than 20 added vetoes allowed to birth parents as they moved to openness.

> *But no matter how, or where, or why the adoption exists, adoptees everywhere should have the absolute, unfettered right to own their heritage and to have full and complete information about their origins, starting with the details of their own particular birth and history. In a just society, this must be an inviolate right of every human being, no exceptions. There should not be a single law anywhere that prevents the adopted from knowing their full truth, as much as can found. International adoption most often piles on a usually insurmountable hurdle for information about one's heritage, and in fact, is the reason that many adopters have turned to other countries to adopt.*

But any law, or agency, or state that restricts full and complete information of one's birth and parentage is a violation of basic human rights and decency. Nothing should annul the right to own one's true identity. No one should ever ask the question of an adoptee: Why do you want to know? That is like asking: Why do you want to be free? As one adoptee wrote on an ABC message board related to a now-canceled show called "Find My Family": "Everybody wants to know where they come from, even if it doesn't turn out like you wanted it."

Indeed, life can change with a single piece of information.

*Today, however, the use of "birth mother" is abhorred by those who see it as an unnecessary obeisance to the past. To them, "birth mother" and "birth child" are attempts to blur the basic natural blood bond between mother and child and to reduce it to a single act: birth. Personally, I avoid the terms whenever possible, but it is not always possible if I am to avoid a kerfuffle and change the tenor of the conversation with someone I want to continue having a dialog with.

"I'm Not Giving Up on Any Adoptee."

The Toll of Adoption on Native Tribes:

~The following is an Excerpt from Trace DeMeyer's One Small Sacrifice: Lost Children of the Indian Adoption Projects:[70]

"Who are you?
Stop and think about this. Who are you?
Think about your parents, your grandparents, and great-grandparents who you knew when you were growing up. Remember the stories of when, where, even how you were born.
Now imagine an adoptee who doesn't know who they are. Nothing, anything, zilch. Can you imagine looking in the mirror, not knowing anything? How might that feel?
A fairytale, you think?
"Adopted people" are the only people in the world without free or unlimited access to their personal histories. We simply vanish into thin air.
This decision, however, was made for us. Someone decided this long ago. Someone decided that adoptees were better off not knowing anything. Someone decided this for me, that I'd be fine with never knowing my own identity.
Wait. I was dead without my identity, without my name. I can't live like this.
My adoptive family had their stories, their names, their parents', and grandparents' names, where they were from, how they lived, died. Everything.
Like them, many people are very proud of their family histories. There

could be bank robbers, or horse thieves, or rich barons, or fancy politicians. To tell my story, I needed more than their story. I needed my own."

* * *

(Note from the editors: While the 2016 President and CEO of Nightlife Christian Adoption Agency alleged on its website that adoption *prevents child trafficking*, he encourages their customer base to shop for a child in South America because of his agency finally having access to Columbian children. At the same time, on the other end of the spectrum, Native American adult adoptees, such as Trace Demeyer, born in 1957, continue to gain attention from anyone willing to listen about recovering from being permanently torn from one's own true identity and culture. Sadly, CEOs of evangelical churches and heads of global satellite congregations have yet to listen and acknowledge the losses involved.)

In *Adoptionland: From Orphans to Activists*, DeMeyer wrote:

> *"But how do I write about Native-American genocide? I ask Indian friends. They say, Well, it's not exactly the Holocaust. It's bigger. Genocide refers to a community of people who were culturally exterminated, wiped out, or literally erased for political or economic reasons.*

Strong words, but true. Some of us are your next-door neighbors. Some of us are incorrectly listed on the census. Some of us are Indian only when we look in the mirror.

There are no photos of when early invaders arrived here and began grabbing land, collecting bounties on Indians, or coordinating military massacres. I didn't see any film footage of the ship that pulled up on Turtle Island, but the story lives on. Indians fought long and hard. Tribes did Winter Counts, a kind of annotated Indian census. Photos and papers exist of Indians signing treaties with white men to commit removals on reservations. I've been to the graveyard from the Wounded Knee Massacre of 1890, the last Indian uprising.

As for the casualties of the Indian adoption projects, I needed a calculator. If the Native American population was two million, and if just one-quarter of all children were removed before the Indian Child Welfare Act of 1978, then, on-paper, 80,000+ children were removed from their families during the early-to-mid-1900s. If the American-Indian population was three million, then over 100,000 babies were removed...

> *I hated this math: This meant that 85 percent of children were removed by adoption in 16 states. That's genocide."*

"Without a Trace," by Native-American author, Trace Demeyer,[71]

Endeavors to civilize the Native Americans were concentrated on the children from Indian tribes and their communities. The 1819 "Civilization Fund Act" was passed by Congress that appropriated funds for agencies, mainly churches, to formulate programs to "civilize the Indian."

Funded by the United States Government, the legislation removed youngsters from their homes and sent them to boarding schools where they were dressed in *civilized* clothing and prohibited from speaking their native languages. The first school opened in Carlisle, Pennsylvania, in 1879.

> *"Transfer the savage-born infant to*

the surroundings of civilization, and he will grow to possess a civilized language and habit."

~ Col. Richard H. Pratt, Founder, Carlisle School

Eventually, the boarding schools were deemed unethical, and adoption was promoted as more humane. The government believed that Native children were better off being raised in White homes. In 1958, the Children Welfare League of America administered the Indian Adoption Project via the Bureau of Indian Affairs to endorse the adoption of Native children by White families.

The policies of the United States assumed that assimilation was the best answer to solve the *problem* of the Native populations and to "save the poor Indian children." Instead of strengthening families, the Indian Adoption Project blatantly stole children from various tribes, viewing the practice as being charitable.

As a consequence, generations of Native American adults have lost connection with their families and communities. To this day, they are forced to cope with little support or resources for the aftermath of unresolved grief and trauma.

Adoption Month

In 1976, Governor Michael Dukakis announced an official Adoption Week for the State of Massachusetts. In 1984, President Reagan proclaimed the first *National* Adoption Week. A decade into the future, President Clinton expanded that week into the *entire month* of November. State and local organizations promote activities to raise awareness about adoption boosting applicants on the campaign that children are *waiting for permanent families.* Some adoptee groups counter the pro-adoption rhetoric, however. Adoptee and human rights groups have pointed out that adopted children are often forced to wait until adulthood to be reunited with siblings and their immediate and extended families. Mirah Riben, author of *The Stork Market*, explained how the phrase "Gotcha Day" (regularly used in adopter circles) can be offensive. She quoted an adopter who admitted to the problematic term in a post titled "The Insensitivity of Adoption Day Celebrations." He conceded that "[a] door home has been slammed shut forever, and the child has been removed from their ancestral home, their blood ties and their language," yet it is still celebrated. Riben, an activist since 1979, recently invited adopted people to explain why "adoption month" might be painful for her column in *The Huffington Post*. The very existence of the article demonstrates how the community's dynamic is slowly shifting from voices belonging only to "private entrepreneurs – adoption attorneys, adoption facilitators, and adoption agency owners and executives" who saw adoption month as an opportunity to hawk their services and run their businesses "under a smokescreen of do-gooder humanitarianism" to (finally) giving a tiny bit of consideration to the individuals who had been adopted as children. Where previously NAAM was used to deluge the public with *happy adoption narratives,* some adopted people are no longer willing to buy into the shame of *abandonment* or the stigmatization of mothers with the label of *unwed*. For example, the evangelical catchphrase *Gotcha Day* when referring to the attainment of children and commonly celebrated by proud adoptive families is now being criticized for being insensitive in the United States.[72] Since American audiences are less likely to buy into the old jargon set by traditionalists, profiteers move onto populations willing to listen and receive their *help*.

Inquiry

In 2012, Maine was the first in the United States to initiate an inquiry. The following year, the Maine Wabanaki State Child Welfare Truth and Reconciliation Commission collected narratives from those who were separated from their families.

"...the life of an adoptee is a lifelong struggle."

"I was made to feel ashamed of my culture."

"My foster mother told me that... nobody on the reservation wanted me."

One elder adoptee of the Passamaquoddy Tribe told of her and her younger sister's wish to "get white" by bathing in a tub of bleach, hoping to then be accepted by their adoptive community.

Esther Attean, MSW, a Passamaquoddy tribal member had this to say about the movement: "My people's continued existence depends on our children being able to be who they are and know who they are. And that transfer of knowledge to generations: cultural knowledge, spiritual knowledge. Those things that make us who we are."

* * *

On searching for the families of Native adoptees, Trace DeMeyer wrote, "I'm Not Giving Up on Any Adoptee." She went on to explain,

"All of these adoptees come from the Indian Adoption Programs and Projects era when the US government and the Child Welfare League of America were funding ARENA (Adoption Resource Exchange of North America) and paying churches and agencies to remove Indian children to purposefully place these babies and children with non-Indian parents in closed adoptions.

Since the late 1800s, these adoptions happened before, during, and after residential boarding schools (in the US and

Canada). It's no surprise that the numbers of adopted Indian children are calculated in percentages, not actual statistics, and left purposefully vague. (Ontario has a class action suit for adoptees in the works. We know First Nations children were also brought from Canada to the US by way of ARENA.) These two governments decided that assimilation was a very good idea because adoptions far from the reservation would somehow erase the Indian blood and a child's memories of home."

She went on to say that with "every phone call I make, I hope to give adoptees something concrete, something helpful, something that will work. In truth, I can't because it doesn't exist, not with sealed adoption records, without paperwork or proof, and current laws that prevent adoptees from knowing their tribal identities.

There are things I want to happen, and my list grows after each call for help. First, I want adoptees and families of loss to write to their legislators and tell them that, 'This is wrong,' until we finally get someone in the government who hears us and offers to help. I want an American government agency to help repatriate adoptees to their tribes. (Canada has three such programs.) I want more people to see this history for what it was: forced assimilation to kill culture in children – a genocide of the mind."

One Small Sacrifice: Lost Children of the Indian Adoption Projects Out of Print. Author (Trace DeMeyer) is now known as Trace Lara Hentz.

* * *

The *genocide* for those in the state of Maine was confirmed by the Wabanaki State Child Welfare Truth and Reconciliation Commission in 2015. Charlotte Bacon, Executive Director of the TRC, delivered its findings to state representatives. Native children were five times more likely to enter foster care than non-Native children between 2002 - 2013. The disproportionate rates of removal, issues of identification, and dispossession (linked with present-day racism) provided "...evidence of continued cultural genocide against Wabanaki people."

First Nation adoptees remaining in the other forty-nine United States still live without any acknowledgment of their losses. And overseas adoptees removed from their home countries have also been unacknowledged by similar governing forces and belief systems that have permanently displaced them and confiscated their identities.

gkisedtanamoogk, from the University of Maine, summed up the losses involved in the documentary, *First Light*, sponsored by the Upstander Project:

> *"It's not just about removing children. It's dismantling everything of their being in the process."*[3]

PART 3:
ORPHAN
PLANES, 1954
ASIA

Setting the Evangelical Stage

*"I became strongly anticommunist;
that was almost my gospel for a while.
That was wrong. I shouldn't have done
that. But that was the way I felt at the
time. I was young and inexperienced.* "[4]

—Reverend Billy Graham on his early years

When discovering that international adoption was expanded exponentially by various religious movements sweeping the world, *sending* countries (as they are referred to by the industry), or one's motherland, can be seen in a whole new light. Christianity in South Korea expanded from an already large group of followers at the end of the Korean War to cleansing away any remnants of indigenous culture. The Reverend Billy Graham, an evangelical Southern Baptist from North Carolina, aided by a dispatch of zealous-minded missionaries like himself, broadcast sermons via satellite. As a result of diligent campaigning, Reverend Graham's vast influence swelled throughout the landscape of the nation and changed it drastically.

To my knowledge, Rev. Billy Graham did not facilitate adoptions, but I believe that adoptioneers throughout history used his dynamism, and his congregation to find applicants. He—similar to other preachers across the world—became convinced that idea was endorsed *by God* by those who initiated and profited from the practice. Therefore, as a consequence, he would later advocate for it (as did many other missionaries). The seeds of advocacy stirred in South Korea in the late 1940s and early 1950s. Just in the United States, the sale of Bibles doubled within five years, and new churches were sprouting across the nation.[75] These churches sent their people across the globe. Evangelist Graham pioneered an expansion of the fundamentalist movement, to include "throwing himself headlong into the public debate, befriending politicians, and discussing social and economic trends, he invited evangelicals to emerge from pious isolation and join him." It is not surprising for him to write a telegram to President Truman in favor of: "Strongly urge showdown with communism now. More Christians in southern Korea per capita than any part of the world. We cannot let them down."[76] Graham's worldwide crusades set the stage for evangelists to gain access, proselytize to the citizens, and influence government authorities using their missionary zeal and charitable work as points of entry. Graham's wife had been educated in Korea while her parents converted and recruited the people of China. In an attempt to put the Korean War in a religious and political perspective, the experiences of Graham's wife allowed for him to be able to weigh in with counsel while Truman served as the United States President. In 1956, the American minister also arrived in Seoul and met publically with South Korea's first President, Syngman Rhee (also a minister), in front of an audience of 50,000 Koreans.

As early as 1947, Reverend Billy Graham would meet with every US president, starting with Harry Truman and on up to George W. Bush. His initial attempt to influence President Truman was to guide him. At their first meeting, young Graham asked Truman "about his personal faith." When Truman replied that he believed in the Sermon of the Mount and tried to live by the Golden Rule, Graham responded, "I don't think that's enough."[77]

No other figure in American history managed to do what this evangelist did. He not only counseled heads of state, but he prayed with them, knew their spouses, their children, and their aides and, according to the book, *The Preacher and the Presidents: Billy Graham in the White House* he played a role in almost every Presidential election between 1952 and 2000.[78] He is believed to have spoken face-to-face with more people in more places than anyone in history, giving sermons to 210 million people in 185 countries throughout the course of 417 crusades.[79]

These crusades were not just one-day events. Most lasted for about a week, but the longest campaign ran sixteen weeks long and took place at Madison Square Garden, a decade after Graham's first. The first campaign, held in 1947, lasted nine days, and assembled six thousand attendees in Grand Rapids, Michigan, at the Civic Auditorium. Since then, the ministry rented stadiums, parks, or entire streets and gathered groups of up to 5,000 singers to set up full choirs from local churches. Inviting large choirs from local areas to perform persuaded family members of the singers to naturally attend the event and for anyone trying to grow the church, resulting in an effective method to increase membership.[80]

"Billy Graham's Evangelical Association (BGEA) used satellite technology to reach the masses and broadcasting became a phenomenal method for the organization to reach millions of followers around the world. The advent of satellite technology opened more doors for BGEA to propagate the Gospel. In 1985 the ministry first used satellites to transmit meetings from Sheffield, England, all over Great Britain. In 1989, the Crusade in London broadcasted live to 250 locations in the United Kingdom and nearly 300 locations across Africa. In 1991, the strategy was expanded in Central and South America, as a Crusade in Buenos Aires was transmitted via satellite and video into 20 Spanish-speaking countries."[81]

Graham's son held his first festival in Alaska and then followed in his father's footsteps with over 160 evangelical festivals worldwide of his own. The crusades were eventually translated into 48 languages and reached the people in San Juan, Puerto Rico. In 2002, he launched My Hope Ministry, garnering more than ten million followers worldwide. A "Rapid Response

Team" deployed to more than "150 disaster zones [for] hurricanes, tornadoes, floods, fires and shootings" allowed for proselytizing to affected nations recovering from these disasters. Some evangelists believed natural disasters were the acts of an angry God, which gave *good people* the right to congregate in the recovery zones and preach.[82]

The Reverend sought to reach the very core of every individual who heard his voice as if he and he alone spoke on behalf of God. *Billy Graham and the Seven Who were Saved,* a published book from 1967, offered an intimate view of the sermons' contents given during the mid-century, tapping into the minister's fierce determination to turn anyone (and everyone) into a *born-again* Christian, harping on the consequences for not obeying:

> *"A lady came here the other night. She was not sure; she was not convinced. She did not come forward. She was still thinking about accepting Jesus as her Savior when she was struck with a heart attack, and life passed out of her body. And so far as I know, she was not reborn, and she must pay the penalty forever— forever! Tonight you have a chance. Why don't you do business with God tonight? He wants you. He loves you. He's patient and He is waiting for you. Come to God tonight in true faith and you live forever!"[83]*

Were such scare tactics used to the Koreans prior to the set up of international adoption? When one reads the words of Korean mothers of adoption-loss decades after the missionary work initiated by Harry Holt, one would answer, *"yes."*

One of the largest Graham Crusades was held in Seoul, South Korea, June of 1973. With the help of a team of volunteers and staff members, he secured Yeoido Park for a five-day event, eventually ending the affair on a humid Sunday. The massive space had previously served as a landing strip during the Korean War. Local officials estimated that the crowd exceeded more than one million Koreans, but over the course of this particular campaign, Mr. Graham spoke to more than three million.[84] Many had waited all night and then through a hot and humid morning.[85] Old video footage shows just how larger than life he appeared to be standing at a podium center stage in front of the receptive citizens of South Korea. The minister started the long and tiresome lectures mentioning his arrival twenty-two years prior in the dead of winter, winning the attention and devotion of the citizens. He instructed them to "love one another—like Jesus did before he died," which reinforced the nation's immersion into the system of belief taught to them by the evangelical leaders of the time.[86]

"A solid block of humanity quietly awaited him. Every section, every aisle between, and away to edges of the plaza hitherto unused, sat an unbroken mass of people, who throughout that service unless singing, stayed incredibly quiet."

Streams of excited Koreans wept openly, appearing to wince, emoting appreciation at Graham's aggressive preaching approach. His interpreter, Dr. Billy Kim, translated the preacher's messages with the same assertive fervor.

Moreover, Graham challenged everyone to stand, "If you're willing to forsake all other gods."

Yet, Korean families did not worship their relatives as *false gods*, as accused by the missionaries when they watched Korean citizens pay their respects to deceased loved ones at altars and graves. Either annually or on the anniversary of a death, relatives reflected on the departed at tombstones, sometimes making small replicas to keep with them. The act of bowing, clasping hands, or crying aloud triggered by heartfelt memories allowed for family members to cherish their loved ones, and mourn the loss; it was not an act of glorification. The missionaries assumed that the citizens were praying to false gods and idols and made them promise to no longer commit such *sins* against God. The missionaries then introduced their own God, Jesus Christ, and handed out Bibles, dropping flyers out of small planes across the rural landscape. Prepackaged food and gospel tracts relaying God's messages falling from the sky? (The natives might have thought that these beings were Gods of some sort!)

One by one, Korean listeners rose until thousands stood to attention. As if on cue, Graham directed the counselors to hand out materials and then guided the mass of people into following his interpretation of the Bible. The ministry collected over 12,000 return postcards on the day of this crusade. Koreans mailed in more and more as the days wore on. "And, as the future showed," according to *The Billy Graham Story*, by John Pollock, "a great many made genuine commitments who never were reached by a counselor at the plaza."[87]

When the helicopter rose from behind the platform, and Dr. Han explained that Billy Graham would be leaving, the Koreans sang more praises.

The aircraft circled over the plaza commemorating the historical movement and "the entire million and more stood and waved their hymn sheets or newspapers or whatever they carried."[88]

The charismatic preacher had won the hearts and minds of South Korea, securing it for future influence. It was during this era that evangelical contemporaries, such as Harry Holt, set up and secured the Overseas Adoption Program, soon to become a normalized welfare scheme, targeting the nation's children under the guise of protection otherwise known as *The Child's Best Interest*.

The reverend was just one of the hundreds-of-thousands of traveling missionaries stationed in Asia intent on saving its citizenry from accused evil practices. He was welcomed and admired like a celebrity—a god. From the day that he landed, native Koreans swarmed him, photographed him, and respected his every move until the day he left on the helicopter. He has made a huge impression on that nation to date. Today, we can see a remnant of the religious ferver. It is not uncommon to be approached by missionaries distributing Bible-based brochures at Korean grocery marts.

While the missionaries claimed that South Koreans persecuted them, millions followed the Southern Baptist's Orthodox teachings. The raising of arms toward the heavens and public displays of emotion expressed the devotion for Graham and other missionaries like him. Soon, Korean philosophies were vilified and wiped from the motherland's national consciousness (as if sinful or inferior).

I remember attending a Billy Graham crusade at Washington State's Tacoma Dome in 1983.[89] Graham drew 24,000 in that one night alone, but these numbers were small in comparison to the almost half-a-million that he attracted to the Seattle Kingdome in 1976 after I was adopted with my twin. This was billed as a very momentous occasion, and those who didn't immediately believe Graham's interpretation of the Bible were stigmatized as *non-believers* in teaching materials or even as *anti-God*. Singing in the massive choir *changed lives* for those who participated, and then seeing the write-up about the event in the local newspaper days later seemed to be another once-in-a-lifetime occurrence. The arena, typically used for sporting events, was filled with eager followers waiting to hear his sermon, which added to the man's celebrity status. The roaring feel-good tune, "Count Me In," backed by the quick fingering of a banjo, and readings of Bible verses set the tone for the stadium event before the Reverend gave his sermon, titled, "Revelations." At crusades past and future, Graham invited listeners to come forward while volunteers distributed Bible study booklets and then prayed with them personally. The "*lost*" were encouraged to dedicate their lives to Jesus and to become a follower for life.

Even today, *unwed* mothers within the crusader culture are expected to relinquish their children, conveniently filling the demand of what previous parents-of-loss now refer to as the child market. Surrendering one's own child is encouraged to win forgiveness, to earn God's love and approval, and to make right the young mother's *sin*. These young women, unfortunately, are encouraged to *do the right thing* and led to believe that they will be invited into heaven for their sacrifice.

Specialized help for pregnant girls continues to be packaged and promoted as "helping people deal with unplanned pregnancies," according to the *700 Club*'s page on the Christian Broadcasting Network website. It is standard practice to send pregnant teens into the homes of those who *know best*, where young mothers (blamed, shamed and made to feel guilty) typically arrive at the decision to relinquish their children. The facility provides care for teen mothers until the babies are born and even offer to pay for medical expenses making the young woman believe that she is even more indebted for the *help*. Unwed mothers are continuously blamed and shamed into relinquishing all rights to their babies, told that the children would be sent to a *better, forever,* and of course, *loving Christian family*. These mothers are then expected to *move on, be thankful* (as if their losses were a good thing), and then claim a successful life without the burden of a child.

Even today, young women are placed under the most scrutiny and the most pressure, given what is coined as *sympathetic* counseling, and then expected to abide by the rules set by the religious authorities. Such attention gives women a false sense of reprieve. Reverend Billy Graham's grand-daughter, seventeen-year-old Windsor Graham, who was initially *adamant that she wanted to keep her baby,* fell under the strain when she became pregnant.[90] Ruth, Windsor's mother (the daughter of Rev. Billy Graham), "felt the best option would be adoption"[91] and then, of course, went on to write a book promoting the practice—as expected when seen from a historic lens.

One can see that the perception of the practice has been warped into the best form of child protection and welfare under the guise of charity. The religious training that *children should be seen and not heard* and *forgiveness* when reaching adulthood allows for these violations to continue, while at the same time prevents young *unwed* mothers from caring for their offspring. Evangelical organizations grabbed the torch to *help* less fortunate nations and, as the saying goes, *ran with it*. Without consulting former families of loss, these charities are on a campaign to rid countries of their orphanages, believing that the group homes and group care are the problems. However, orphanages provide necessary services for families, even offering communities temporary shelters, care centers, boarding schools, hospices, hostels, and nursing homes (for infants and babies). The orphanage facilities were not built specifically to house children to be reserved for foreign missionaries to pull from for export overseas. However, many facilitators were on a mission to accomplish exactly this.

Armed with the idea to further operations, some wonder if the Holts befriended and influenced the first President of South Korea and his Austrian-born wife, to provide an air of legitimacy and justify their *charitable* needs and reputation. Was Syngman Rhee, also a minister, used to fulfill Harry Holt's dream? After all, South Korea's first president was highly respected in the United States. He graduated in 1907 from George Washington University, obtained a master's degree from Harvard University, and earned his Ph.D. from Princeton University in 1910. He returned to Korea as a Presbyterian minister and evangelist and married an Austrian woman, who would then become the First Lady of South Korea. The couple met when she translated for him while working at the League of Nations in Geneva. Syngman Rhee proposed to her in Austria, and they married in New York in 1934.[92] Mr. Rhee became South Korea's very first President in March of 1948, served three terms, and held the office until 1960. He and his wife went on to adopt a boy. During this era, the Holts set the stage for their global adoption program. Rhee's acquisition of a child is suspected to have influenced by dinner meetings and other socializing with the Holts introducing and recruiting the program of overseas adoption. In any event, the enthusiastic couple's missionary zeal would eventually pave the way for routinely exporting children from South Korea as if conjured up by and ordained by God and not dreamed up by Harry Holt, a fallible and imperfect man.[93]

Hammering Down Adoption Culture

This chapter was researched in the honor and remembrance of the Holts' Korean-born ward, Joseph Tae Holt (1952 – 1984), who committed suicide inside their Oregon home at the age of 32, and other Korean-born adoptees deprived of their Korean families.[94]

Studies today indicate that adoptees are four times more likely to commit suicide than the non-adopted.[95]

Does staying *positive*—like we're scolded to do—and dismissing human rights violations (while treating the families left behind as if they do not exist) sabotage progress? Somehow, someway, nature will repair itself, and justice will be served.

***

From 1954 and continuing to this day, more than 200,000 South Korean children have been forced to abandon their true identity and instead to adapt overseas in foreign homes by way of intercountry adoption. When evangelicals Harry and Bertha Holt first scouted the area,[96] South Korea did not have a word for adoption, and many mothers did not understand that adoption meant "a clean break or forever."[97]

On December 14, 1954, Harry Holt, also a successful mill owner and farmer, watched *Dead Men Furlough*,[98] produced by Bob Pierce of World Vision, Inc. The purpose of the film was to increase donations from fellow Christians for their sponsorship programs against the potential threat of spreading Communism. The scratchy black-and-white film inspired Mr. Holt to travel to South Korea, which he did so with the approval and support of his wife, Bertha, (also a first cousin) and their six (biological) children.

Initially, Mr. Holt gathered eight Korean-born Amerasian children to be *his* children at the Holt farm in Creswell, Oregon. For this, the media descended upon the family, and as a consequence, the Holts received acclaimed national attention. Fellow evangelists immediately fell in love with the idea of overseas adoption, and the Holt family became known all throughout the United States as *child saviors*. This advanced their initiative to transport children from Asia to all parts of the Western world. Bertha explained in a letter to one of her orphans, "We were deluged with inquiries on how to adopt children, so my husband returned to Korea and started an adoption agency. He was helped by our Senator in Wash[ington] and learned the laws how they could adopt by proxy, and the parents would not have to go to Korea."

The U.S. Children's Bureau, the Child Welfare League of America, and the American Branch of International Social Services at first accused Bertha and Harry Holt of devising an unethical, international mail-order child racket hiding behind a charitable veneer. However, because of the Holts' friendship with Senator Neuberger, state representatives, and several other government officials, they were able to quickly obtain permanent visas for the Korean-born children under an extended Refugee Relief Act that, under normal circumstances, might have taken two or three years to obtain. Soon after they received permission, the Holts processed Amerasian children by the hundreds. Each week, fellow Christians visited the Holts farm in Creswell, Oregon. The primary interest was to "see what the children looked like." Soon, Americans and friends were begging for children.

The following year, as early as December 21, 1955, Harry submitted a proposal called "Adoption by Proxy," to the director of the visa office. Adoption by Proxy gave Harry legal guardianship of the children, permitting him to *legally* send children overseas. The Holt memoir described how the procedure "cut out the red tape" and was considered "cheaper and quicker." Proxy adoptions were perceived to be a Christian triumph against the United States Government.[99] At the time, the Holts viewed the government to be one of the biggest impediments to getting Korean children to their *rightful* families in America. Laws had not yet been established between the two nations to process the children efficiently. Proxy adoptions allowed for Christian clients to give power of attorney to Harry Holt, who then represented their clients' desires under Korean law. This way, their clients no longer had to travel overseas to acquire their purchases, which was fantastic news for those who wanted a child but were themselves unwilling to travel to the nations they feared.

The Holts shipped the children to the United States as *sons* and *daughters* for the affluent couples. Determined to fill the wishes of scores of fellow Christians, the Holts set up a compound in Seoul, hoping to find more *orphans*. By Christmas of 1955, they had already received thousands of inquiries from couples and ministers. One missionary, stationed in Japan, wrote to the Holts that he was "deeply interested in the 4,000 or more Amerasian children." Bertha mentioned that the pastor "was pleased [the Holts] were endeavoring to place those little fellows into Christian homes."

In a ceremony in February of 1956, the Rev. Billy Graham blessed Harry Holt's Seoul-based Child Reception Center, and the Holts started receiving over 50 letters daily and applications from couples in every state (except for Maine and Rhode Island).

***

The Holt Adoption Program is a global operation and currently hailed as the most professional and ethical of all adoption agencies—at least within the leaflets of its promotional marketing material designed for potential applicants. Despite initial objections by the U.S. Government, the organization has forged ahead. In her memoir *Bring My Sons From Afar,* Bertha Holt wrote that as early as April 28, 1956, the American Social Agency denounced proxy adoptions "furiously"[100] after a visit to her home and office. However, future networking with government officials prompted a change in some of the laws, which would allow for a sanctioned migration.

The warm, welcoming embrace of White couples adoring Asian babies helped to present the Holts and their evangelical followers as good people, especially since race relations were strained in the United States. Pastors across America and Europe promoted the idea fervently to their flocks. During the 1950s and 1960s, many congregations loved the idea of adopting a child. Families made by adoption were judged to be moral and *better* in comparison to conventional families. Overseas adoption also provided the added benefit of not having to contend with the foreign parents or their inferior culture according to applicants. Every Christian who adopted a baby enjoyed the reputation of *tolerating* other races. Taking the child out of its cultural environment benefitted the new clients, too. What appeared to be progressive attracted additional followers and allowed for *good Christian families* to legally proselytize to other people's children. The integration of these minority children into these good Christian homes created an air of moral superiority in the minds of these clients. Unlike with the domestic adoption of White children, clients could stroll around with *Asian* children and instantly be noticed, producing special attention and an opportunity to testify their religious beliefs. Intercountry adoption grew to become an acceptable practice for long-term recruitment.

"Orphans are a no-no in the Orient,"

According to Bertha Holt who wrote to one of her processed "orphans" in 1994. "*A child without a family is destitute. No one will marry him, he is a disgrace, because Orientals are very family oriented. You were abandoned because twins are thought to be a curse. And we [evangelicals] think they are a double blessing. We have many calls for twins...*" The adoption-pioneer went on to admit in what felt like a self-righteous tone:

> *"Their Oriental customs are different from ours. The Eugene office has processed about 70,000 children and are now in 16 countries from where we get children."*

Undeterred from any interference and completely trusted by followers, Harry sent Korean children to families he deemed more appropriate, willing, and able (namely American families), despite the problem that the Holt Adoption Program would "weaken the monopoly on American babies." At that time, he separated from World Vision since the child-sponsor organization did not export children with the intention to facilitate as many foreign adoptions to the United States *as the Lord will allow.*

Adoption laws passed in the West were designed to make obtaining a child easier. Westerners became indoctrinated by the adoption rhetoric, which asserted that intercountry adoption was as *Godly* as giving birth. The *successful* child welfare programs that claimed to send children to *better* homes were similar to the child migration schemes initiated in the United Kingdom and New York. Competition for Asian children grew vicious.

Harry Holt wrote to Bertha,

> *"We have trouble finding the little ones, other agencies are grabbing them,*

and some aren't released by mothers.[101]

Within the first year, the Holts' popularity exploded in their favor nationwide, although they were also struggling with increased competition and difficulty finding adoptable children. By air, they dropped more leaflets and gospel tracts on Korea's rural areas enticing the citizens to serve God and to send them children to be *saved*. At first, the missionaries targeted mothers of mixed-race children. The mothers heeded their offers of assistance, and babies were relinquished by what was termed *a loving choice*.

***

The Holts built a commune in Korea, which served as an orphanage to gather, rename, and process children while, on the other side of the globe, their helpers attracted and approved applicants eager to acquire those children. Before sending the children off, they dressed the tiny tots in Western clothing, as if they were getting them ready for Sunday School, but to be photographed for prospective Westerner buyers. One could assume that this method kept the applicants excited and engaged and probably inspired more donations. Once the children arrived in their newly-assigned homes, they were denied accurate portrayals of their Korean families and their home country. If the children did not abide by the house rules, the guardians used corporal punishment to *correct* them. The primary hope was to proselytize, giving the children a *good Christian* upbringing. On the other hand, the well-being of the parents and families left behind in Korea was never considered. The Holts focused solely on uprooting Korean children for fellow Christian couples, using marketing tactics among their networks across the United States. These are still used today.

Because of the American media attention, including articles in *Life Magazine* and *Reader's Digest*, the Holts received letters and daily applications from almost every single state in the union.

They used this national interest to publicize their devout Christianity. Their mission touched and motivated followers at their core.

The Holts felt it was crucial to give the Korean-born Amerasian (half-American and half-Korean) children *only* to other Christians. In America, however, the children were not welcomed, particularly in rural areas. The tenacious missionaries received more than a few threats, including phone calls accusing the family of bringing back "slant-eyed monsters," as the vast nation still struggled with both blatant and covert racism. However, the accolades from clients, senators, representatives, ministers, government ministries, and presidents countered most objections. It was generally assumed that the practice of adoption was a nonracist act, and the children would grow up grateful to have been *saved*. The idea that adopted individuals might one day see the practice as an egregious loss of connection with their families and indigenous cultures meant next to nothing in this line of work.

***

The South Koreans fully trusted that their children would be well-taken care of, believing the assurances from agency representatives that every child would be sent to a *forever family* managed by *loving Christians*. However, for many adult adoptees looking back on their upbringings, such agency slogans are now perceived as superficial and inexcusable, promoting a form of modern-day neocolonialism and cultural genocide to the children who never asked to have their identities altered. Peter Dodds, a German-born intercountry adoptee, and researcher, who first spoke out against intercountry adoptions and a proponent on the United Nations Convention on the Rights of the Child, agrees. His published paper, comparing transnational adoption to slavery, and can be found on the digital commons at Providence College online.[102] At the very least, the adoption industry was built on false information and deception.

Harry Holt pitched the idea of American exceptionalism to

struggling Korean moms and government officials. At one time, he advised Bertha to hide a photo of one of the little Korean adoptees sitting on a lawn barefooted at one of their family picnics in Oregon.

"Never let anyone in Korea see the picture." If someone saw it, he feared the Koreans would assume there was not enough money to buy shoes for the children. Harry assured the Koreans that the children would receive better care in the States. As followers of the Christian faith, the Koreans admired their American counterparts, even making the assumption that adoptees were living busy lives and "did not want to be bothered." As a consequence, Korean mothers were discouraged from "disturbing" their children sent abroad and were not allowed to know their new names or to have any contact with them according to adoption law.

Within four years of Harry's arrival in South Korea in the winter of 1959, Mr. Holt's compound had grown to 7000 square feet and included multiple buildings. Prospective clients flooded the Holts with phone calls, and nothing seemed to slow the momentum of their adoption program, not even articles reporting unethical adoption cases or reports about the deaths of adopted children. Instead, the Holts bragged that controversy actually brought an avalanche of inquiries from interested people.

Mrs. Holt once boasted that fifty Korean employees had to be trained to keep up with demand.

> *When Harry scoured the countryside the same winter, the Holt's daughter wrote that their Korean liaison "did a good job of talking to mothers."*

Eighty-five children had already died within the compound by 1959. Many of the deaths could have been prevented if parents had been permitted inside the commune to see their children. In 1964, ten years after the Holts first became determined to fulfill Harry's dream, the charity ran out of requests for children from interested Christians. They decided *not* to end their activities, but rather accepted fees and, reluctantly, gave *non-Christians* permission to adopt.

In 1994, Bertha wrote to one of her previous so-called orphans that she prayed daily for "every child we process will become a Christian." She credited their own successful adoptions, compared to all the other adoption agencies, had been due to the Holts Christian status since they "prayed constantly for wisdom in placing children." She admitted that "[o]ther agencies tried to stop us, but eventually they incorporated overseas adoption into their [strategy]."

Special interest groups and lobbyists continued working on expanding the practice, convincing other nations to use permanent intercountry-adoption placements to create their families, hailing them as the "loving option." Industry builders decided that Koreans should *not* provide for their children in their own country, but should ship them overseas.[103] Less severe solutions that kept families together and offered the potential of reunions have been regularly dismissed, even though the Korean War ended more than sixty years ago.

Today, the pioneering Holt Adoption Program purports to be the most ethical and prominent agency in the world. Investigative reporter, Kathryn Joyce, and author of *The Child Catchers: Rescue, Trafficking, and the New Gospel of Adoption, mentions that adoptions from Korea* is considered a Cadillac version. In other words, the industry refers to adoptions from Korea as *top of the line.* Inspired by the Holt family's fearlessness, adoption programs have expanded to almost every nation on earth. The same rhetoric focusing on children languishing and withering away inside orphanages has been used worldwide to rationalize tearing apart families. Such rhetoric builds empathy for the charity, increases potential funds, and justifies the actions and policies of child services. Matching and processing are allowed, but Korean citizens are prevented from making their own decisions. In the case of child protection, religion and politics have become one and the same.

In addition to donations, many of Holt's customers put unwavering faith and trust in the developing adoption empire.

Marketing efforts presented glorified images of adoption in both the East and the West. For example, a cartoon titled "Fairy Tale," written by Chang-Shin Lee and illustrated by Young-bum Yoon for a Holt publication portrayed adoption as something sanctioned by God. Comic strips depicted the system in the most simplistic of terms, presenting Korean babies as destined to be gifted to white couples overseas. In one such rendering, childish-looking balloons presented the following verbiage: "God made a child," "God looked for a family to give this child to," "one day he found one," and "God gave the baby as a gift to that family." "[Western] Mom and Dad were so happy to receive this baby as a gift." "Mom, Dad, and Baby were all so happy." References to the Bible planted the adoption program into the minds of their followers and secured them into a lifetime of loyalty and gratitude.

However, according to the most current survey results as of this writing, which was initiated by Adoption Truth & Transparency Worldwide Network (one of the largest adoptee-led social media groups on Facebook), 100% of all respondents consisting of only adult adoptees, do not believe that God planned and arranged adoptions—as implied by evangelical adoption facilitators—but that *adoptions are planned and initiated by humans.*

The Chosen One

The evangelicals claimed culture had little value and that a *relationship with Christ* was what mattered most when discussing other people's children. This and the myth that the children were *unwanted* by Korean society motivated the evangelists to find and collect as many children as possible. When one digs deeper, evidence shows Korea to be one of the first nations to serve as a training ground due to the exceptionally welcoming, modest, and trusting inhabitants. When the missionaries (like Harry Holt) arrived, David Hyungbok Kim wanted very much to cooperate.

When David first met the adoption pioneer, Mr. Holt, the young Korean man, who was first hired as an interpreter, explained that his Korean grandfather and father were Presbyterian pastors. Therefore, the prospect of working for the Holts was considered a privilege by his entire family.

David said of the time, relaying his excitement, "The possibility of helping war orphans captivated me. I formed a mental picture of this saintly man [Harry Holt] who wanted to help children left homeless by the war. That night I could hardly sleep, even though I had spent a long day at work and school."

Mr. Kim respected the Americans very much for making certain sacrifices, which to him and to other Korean citizens, "secured freedom and democracy" in South Korea. "Now [the Americans] wanted to adopt our war orphans as their sons and daughters! I asked myself, 'Are they some kind of saints?'"

Though nervous and unsure of what to expect prior to training, Hyungbok remembered, "the hope of helping thousands of orphans outweighed my apprehensions." He soon embarked on something new that "seemed unprecedented."

Hyungok Kim learned how to go out into the field and proselytize to mothers, which led to convincing government officials to permit Holt to send children overseas (as if born to the foreign clients). This practice continues to this day after generations, and Mr. Kim eventually became President of Holt International Children's Services.

The pioneers' priority was to establish an office in the early 1950s, to continue public relations work, convince the Korean public to relinquish their rights, and send their mixed-race children to Christian families as if an opening to be blessed by God for doing so. Every day, staff explained the program, met with reporters, visited radio stations for interviews, and established contacts with their overseas partners: evangelical communities, churches, and government offices.

David explained how Mr. Holt "spent most of his time visiting the front lines and the U.S. military bases, talking with the mothers of mixed-race children." He told them, "there was little time left." Presented as an opportunity, David wrote in his book *Who Will Answer*, published by Holt International in 2006: "We printed tracts introducing the Holt Adoption Program. One side of the tract urged relatives of mixed-race children not to delay; otherwise, this opportunity might not be available after the law expired at the end of the year. On the other side of the tract was a gospel message, urging mothers to change their lifestyle and become Christians."[104]

The Holt staff "printed these tracts by the thousands, distributed them to churches, stores, orphanages, and railroad and bus stations. Mr. Holt thought it was an excellent opportunity for us to spread the Good News to people who did not believe in God. Our staff carried a few hundred tracts with them whenever they traveled."

Soon the Korean public held the Holts in the same high regard as Hyungbok Kim aka *David*.

David Kim needed visas for more than one hundred children, and this worried him. "Everyone in the consular section was surprised to see me bring two suitcases full of visa applications and the required supporting documents." He shared fond memories of working as a trainee under Harry Holt's guidance in a published book by the Holt organization.

Mr. Holt, the initiator of international adoptions, refused to take *no* for an answer. He bullied Koreans into compliance, including those who worked in the embassy. Once, when Harry got impatient at the Korean Vice-Consul, Mr. Holt even attempted "punch him [the dignitary] in the face. Luckily the vice-consul retreated, and Mr. Holt missed him, but his fist landed on a thick ashtray on the desk, exploding it into several pieces, sending ashes and cigarette butts flying everywhere. His hand bled from the broken glass. Everyone in the office was stunned, gazing at the two men facing each other."

When David was told that Harry Holt had attempted to punch the Korean Vice Consul in the face at the embassy but missed, Holt's Korean assistant could not believe it. The man assumed Mr. Holt was "too kind, humble, and incapable of doing such a thing." However, later he discovered that *it was true*.

While Harry Holt was referred to as a *terrifying man* by Koreans working in government, the missionary merely chuckled, "Korean people trying to exercise their two-bit authority," referring to South Korea's embassy staff. Harry Holt "was not afraid of government officials," after all, he claimed he was working for God. The children were billed as-if-born-to evangelical Americans simply by filling out an application and paying the required fees.

But, prior to social media and due to the infatuation with the idea of adoption, and ignoring the fact that children would be permanently severed from their families, the Korean trainee and interpreter proudly exclaimed, "Thereafter, the U.S. Embassy always provided excellent service for our children. I understood how Mr. Holt became a successful businessman. He could do things no ordinary men could do! Over the next few weeks, the embassy issued us nearly one hundred visas."

When Holt trainee and interpreter, Mr. Kim, returned to the United States Embassy, to his relief, he noticed the Vice-Consul had been replaced! This way, could he submit numerous visa requests without delay? In addition, Holt trainee noticed the Consul staff treated him cordially and respectfully. The issuance of hundreds of visas continued without further problems. Not only did Harry Holt win the trust (or fear) of Korean Government officials, but he trained and recruited additional Korean staff, and adult adoptees, to travel to Vietnam, India, Brazil, and numerous other countries to win access to more of the world's children. Most recently, since critical adult adoptees have made public complaints against Holt International, the organization changed their public image to claim that they *uplift children, strengthen* and *preserve families*, and even collect donations to *fight against child trafficking*. Parents are even more disgusted with the agency's deceptive public-image update that gives the impression that they care for, and *empower*, the families who are left behind. Many informed human rights proponents believe that these organizations have weakened the family structure and jeopardized its future well being. Until the concerns of formerly manufactured *orphans* are adequately addressed, we recommend placing a moratorium on the practice to best protect all families at risk of exploitation. Much to the dismay of adult adoptees who work to curb the crisis of adoption trafficking, the President of the Hague accredited Nightlight Christian Adoptions even stated on February 1st, 2016, that "Adoption Prevents Trafficking."[105] His claim was in direct opposition to what previous manufactured orphans turned activists have been trying to warn the public about for years: That at the very least, the practice of overseas adoption has created a demand for children and allowed for profits to be made through sanctioned networks of wholesalers and retailers.

***

Out of great respect for the Americans, Hyungbok Kim refused to disobey orders or to speak ill of Mr. Holt. He believed that God chose Harry. "It was impossible for me to imagine what God had in store when I first began working with Mr. Holt. As time went on, it became obvious God had chosen Mr. Holt to initiate the Holt Adoption Program in Korea, and for me to carry on the mission with him in Korea."

Mr. Kim held Harry Holt in the highest regard. The Korean man went on to become Associate Director and led the pioneering adoption agency to where it is today. He wrote of Mr. Holt that he was a *self-made* man who "...had only an eighth-grade education, but was a genius in practical matters." Despite having a "violent temper," Harry (according to David), was "quick to repent and apologize for his mistakes."

Mr. Kim answered he would do his best for as long as he was needed or until Harry relieved him from the position.[106] In April of 1964, the pioneer of intercountry adoption suddenly died of a heart attack, at age 59, at the orphanage he owned and operated.[107] By this time, Hyunbok referred to Holt as his "best friend, mentor, and brother." Hyungbok believed that he must continue the mission to be accepted into the gates of Heaven. In the last paragraph of his memoir, Hyungbok wrote, "Ultimately we must strive to work as Harry Holt did."[108]

Orphan Fever

Excerpt From
*Adoptopia: A Deep Dive Into the Life and Times of Adoptive Father,
The Reverend Jim Jones**

**Jim Jones is also known as the Cult Leader who led the Jonestown
massacre on November 18, 1978. This dramatization is based on the FBI
audio of when he received the first two of three Korean children from the
evangelical church—on a stage of all places and broadcasted by satellite radio
all over the world. The adoptions of these children were presented as the most
beautiful action—as if God had given them instructions to take in the
children.*

***

As part of a decades-long ministry, radio and television
minister Reverend Fred Jordan interviews several sets of adopters
who are about to receive children they have selected from South
Korea through the "Church in the Home" program. Among the
waiting couples are Reverend Jim and Marceline Jones, who
receive – and meet for the first time – two children who became
known as Stephanie and Lew Jones. The following is adapted
from a FBI audio-recording transcription.

From the sidelines, a television spokesman makes an
announcement, commencing the day's special October 1958
production: "This worship service, *Church in the Home*, is brought
to you each week from our radio and television chapel in Los
Angeles, California."

A crew pointing large television cameras places the spotlight on the announcer. "*Church in the Home* is offered as a public service across America to foreign countries and to our armed forces around the world."

Sporting a three-piece suit, Reverend Fred Jordan jumps onto the stage, marches to the center, grabs hold of, and speaks into a stand-mounted microphone, offering a morning salutation. "Greetings to all of our friends and members of *Church in the Home* throughout this great nation of ours and wherever you may be watching television or viewing this telecast... God bless each and every one of you. ...We have, as I indicated in my prayers, some special guests, little ones all the way from the land of Korea. And your friends who've prayed and who have cooperated and been so wonderful in sponsoring this one orphanage that we sponsor in Korea, are going to see the little – just a little bit of the fruit of your prayers and your gifts and your efforts."

> *A beautiful melody from a golden harp and an organ sweep through the air, and the audience sings to the tune of, Holy, Holy, Holy, Lord God Almighty. There are more cheering and applause from the approving viewers. Arms are raised toward heaven. Eyes are shut soaking in the gospel. The group is unified by echoing Hallelujahs. The music dies down and then softens.*

The Reverend introduces a horn-rimmed woman in a coachman's dress, "We have one of God's angels here today. I thought a long time last night before I decided to use that expression. In our hospitals, we call our nurses 'angels of mercy,' but I think if you could watch this young lady in her directing and operating this orphanage, I think you'd be like the little lady I met today who has five little babies. And she was feeling quite weary and tired, and I said, 'How would you like to have twenty-two little babies in a crib in one room?' 'Well,' she said, 'I guess I have a lot to be thankful for.' This is the director that you sent out over four years ago to our orphanage that we built and supported there."

Lorraine Jost, the show's special guest and orphanage owner, arrived at the airport the day before, towing four small children from South Korea. Church leaders, radio, and news crews anticipated this arrival and wiped the sweat from their brows, not really sure what they were doing, but excited to work "for the Lord," also realizing that there would be an adjustment for the children who would be received by folks speaking a foreign language. The fog had delayed the landing of the plane at the international airport. Thrilled Americans impatiently waited to receive the babies they had paid the traveling expenses for and prayed for long and hard.

Rev. Jordan swung into full gear, expertly captivating his live audience. "Our God and our Heavenly Father, we thank thee for your son, Jesus Christ, who said, Suffer the little children to come unto me and forbid them not, for such is the kingdom of Heaven. We thank thee for these precious little darlins that have come to us today as our guests from the far-off land of [South] Korea. We pray that you'll bless them, bless these parents who're filled with all kinds of emotions as they receive today the new little babe that's going to go home with them to distant states and to become their very own. In the name of that same Christ, we pray. Amen."

"Amen," the crowd nodded.

Soon four Korean children would be doled out in three different directions. Rev. Jordan prepared the audience. "We're going to see you several times today on this program and the babies, we want you to present them to the parents. I know it's going to be a ... a terrific emotional hour for all of us as the parents receive these precious little dolls all the way from Korea."

Against the backdrop of organ music, Rev. Jordan welcomed and addressed the crowd. "We know that you're going to have a real thrill when we present that little baby. We'll do that in just a few minutes to all you parents, but first, now I want us to listen to the harp as Harriet plays."

Harriet strums the heart-shaped harp on cue, and the melody is accompanied by an old pipe organ. The melody sounds saintly to the congregation.

"Thank you, Harriet. And, you know, when Jesus picked up that little baby in His arms and said of such is the Kingdom of Heaven," Rev. Fred says, affectionately, "I think there must've been some rejoicing in Heaven. And I'm sure that there was yesterday when this plane arrived with these little babies from Korea and their parents were there ready to greet them. And one of the parents came here from Denver, Colorado, Mrs. Braden. And she's our guest today, and she's going to receive a little baby to take home to her husband and the family back in Denver. And so all you friends in Denver, uh, get on the phone right now and call your neighbors and tell them to tune in and maybe you'll know Mrs. Braden, your neighbor. Mrs. Braden, will you come here to the pulpit? And I want to find out why you wanted this little baby from Korea," the televangelist asks. "Uh– First of all, uh, you're married–"

Mrs. Braden nods. "Yes, sir."

Rev. Fred presumes, "–and you have a husband–"

"Yes."

"And what does your husband do?"

Mrs. Braden brightens. "He's in the real estate business."

"Real estate business."

"Mm-hmm."

"Now, do you work?"

"No, I'm a housewife."

"You're a housewife. Well, that'll be wonderful." Rev. Fred approves. "You have any children?"

"Uh–." The woman turns suddenly bashful. "No."

"No, children," the good minister repeats.

"I have one now!" she laughs.

"You have one now!" Rev. Fred loves the woman's positivity. "You're going to have one in a few minutes. We're going to give you one from Korea. Now what-what prompted you to, uh, uh, contact us about uh, uh, adopting a child from our orphanage?"

"Well, in your paper – Of course, you featured them every now and then, and a lady from our church who receives your paper gave us the information."

The Reverend holds up one of his brochures. "Oh, it's probably like this paper here that's, uh, orphans."

"Yes," Mrs. Braden nods.

"Or something like that?" Rev. Fred guesses, referring to the verbiage on the flyer.

"Yes."

"Well, we'll be happy for folks to get a copy. It'll tell them about the orphanage work and, uh, then you corresponded with us–"

"We wrote right away," Mrs. Braden interrupted, "and we've just been anxious ever since to hear."

> *"Well, the people that sponsor these orphans in our orphanages in Japan and Korea, they're anxious that they become Christians and reared in Christian homes."* The televangelist asks, *"You and Mr. Braden Christian people?"*
>
> *"Oh, yes."* Mrs. Braden stands a little straighter.
>
> *"And you'll believe in the Lord with all your heart?"* asks the minister.
>
> *"I certainly do."*
>
> *"You intend to bring up the child that way?"*
>
> *"Oh, definitely."*

In the background, more pipe organ music reverberates. Three lovely females croon a song about Jesus as Christ. The

Reverend stands aside, allowing for the ladies to have the full spectrum of attention from the audience perched, arena-style, who surround the stage.

"Thank you, girls. Nice to see you again."

On cue, the singers nod and exit the stage, and the television crew pushes forth an eloquent couple. The man is tall, has all-American good looks, and distinct charm. His name is Reverend Jim Jones, and he already knows how to attract a crowd. His wife, Marceline Jones, is poised next to him.

> *"And now we have a minister and his wife here from back east and, uh, we're so happy to have them receive two children from our orphanage today. And, uh, I want them to come right now, Mr. and Mrs. Jones.*

God bless you. Mrs. Jones, I under– God bless you, Mr.–Reverend Jones, and I understand that, uh, you're a registered nurse."

"Yes, I am," says Marceline Jones. (At this time, she is unaware of her one-month pregnancy with a son.)

Rev. Fred: "Is that right?"

Marceline nods. "That's right."

Rev. Fred points to Lorraine, waiting out of camera range, clutching the hands of Chioke,[109] a two-year-old Korean boy, and Stephanie, a four-year-old girl. "Well, Lorraine Jost, our director is a–a registered nurse, and I know that's going to be a big help with those children."

Marceline, "Yes, it has been already."

"Don't you kind of, uh, uh, spend part of your time ministering to the sick?"

Marceline nods. "Yes, uh, our church has a nursing home, a home for the aged, and I work as administrator–"

"Well, isn't that wonderful!" the reverend exclaims.

Marceline adds, "–in an advisory capacity."

"Uh, this pastor and his– his church and his lovely wife

operate a–a home for the aged. Isn't that right?"

Mrs. Jones nods. "That's right."

Rev. Fred brings Jim Jones closer in. "And the needy, and we're so glad, and– and Mr.– uh, I want to call you, "Long," but it's Jones. I don't know why I want to call you Reverend Long, but uh, I wonder if you could give us just a little of your background, how you got into the – the ministry, and something about your church, we're interested in, and your work back there. Surely your hands are full! This lady directs a home for the aged, her husband has a church, and he operates it without salary. He receives no salary. Is that right?"

"Correct," Jones assures.

"And you make, you...you have your other income from other sources?" Rev. Fred asks. "And so, how did you get into all of this, and now you want two babies?"

"Just a desire to help people primarily is the reason," Jones says, matter of factly. "We've had a great interest in breaking down barriers between all races and nations and creeds, and that's the primary reason, Brother Jordan, we have, uh, entered into the field."

"I see."

"We've certainly been pleased to come in contact with your work." Jim Jones continues, "We might say that when we were looking for children, we went to different agencies, and all of them had such fabulous prices connected with the adoption part, and your agency had no charge, it was just merely the transportation of the children, and you were interested in the welfare of the human being. We felt we wanted to tell that to the television audience."

"Well, thank you so much," says Rev. Jordan, taken slightly aback. "Uh, we didn't ask for that, but we certainly appreciate it, because people just imagine that it's a black market and you're making a fabulous sum of money. And, uh, you know why we want to adopt [out] children? We want them to have a normal home, that's one thing. Especially with, uh, Christian parents, and love, but we also want another thing. We want to vacate our orphanage as fast as we can, to receive those who are dying on the streets, and that are taken to the city hall, ten or fifteen a day, the city hall there in Seoul, Korea, no place to go. And all the orphanages are full and running over and beyond capacity, and you're taking two will make it possible for us, uh, to receive some more orphanages– uh, orphans."

"That's right," Rev. Jones said.

"And it's so wonderful to have you here, and we'll put those two little babies in your arms in just a...a few minutes."

Reverend Fred Jordan motions for Lorraine to prepare the Korean children...."

PART 4: ORPHAN TRAFFICKING, TODAY AFRICA

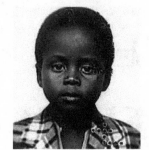

In memory of Manasseh

"As a child, I was told that I was adopted because my Haitian mother could not afford to raise me. I then become the little black guy with whom the other white students of the school do not want to play. My revolt is silent. From the outside, I offer the appearance of a quiet, obedient, docile kid. But inside, it's bubbling, it's swirling. The little Haitian I am in my heart, can't thrive."

Manasseh aka Tinan Leroy,
Adoption Stories collected by Janine Myung Ja,
& *Adoptionland: From Orphans to Activists*,
Adopted from Haiti to France in 1984.
Died of heart failure in 2014.

Dead Girl Walking

Special Contribution by Mae Claire | Adopted from Haiti to United States:

One of the scariest things about adoption is that we adoptees don't really know our history. We don't know where we come from, who we really belong to, and what our future will look like due to the above thoughts.

I was adopted back in 1987 by two white supremacists who, on the outside, looked loving, kind, and gentle. But, on the inside the privacy of the adoptive home, spewed words of hate, racism, and superiority to anything and anyone who was not of their hue. So growing up, I always felt like the "other." I was that person they hated so much.

I constantly heard out of my adoptive mother's mouth, "Black people are this way; black people do that." I knew that I would be classified as one of them and I wouldn't be welcomed if I did not "talk proper." My adoptive parents didn't directly say, "White people are better," but sometimes in the not saying, you say too much....

When I was about ten years old, I started to develop faster than my sister. During the time I was living with them, they told me that I was the same age as their biological daughter. Up until I was about ten, we were the same height, about the same weight and the same pudginess. I really had no reason to doubt their claim.

It wasn't until I was a little over ten that I started to develop breasts. I started asking them, "why, if we are the same age, am I developing at a faster rate than she is?" Today we know that so many factors could have caused this, but what my adoptive parents failed to do was actually care about me and what my papers said.

Instead of looking at my birth certificate, they went with their "fantasy." It was clear on the birth certificate that I was older than she was by about three years, and no one EVER said a word. Why? Did they want to continue what they had started? Did they want to keep pretending that I was white, like them, that I would always weigh the same as she did, and that I would always be a "happy baby?" Growing up as a black child in a mainly white family was very detrimental. I didn't know I was actually black until I had turned about seven or eight years of age. No one really told me I was "black." But, it gets worse. No one ever told me that I was dead either. There is a feeling of loss that comes with being adopted. It is not just a feeling. It is a reality. One loses trust, and one learns to not care anymore. And, there is even a more profound feeling of despair when you realize that everything you were taught to be (maybe) true, is not even a little bit true. For the longest time, I thought my name was what it was on my birth certificate.

When I become a teenager, my adoptive parents finally came somewhat clean and revealed that I was actually not who I thought I was. My name was actually NOT what it was on my birth certificate, that I was older than they told me I was, and that I was actually DEAD!

In Haiti, it is very hard to retrieve documents from the archives because back in the 70s and 80s documents were not recorded on computers. Things were kept by hand, stored drawers or boxes, and forgotten. When my biological mother dropped me off at the orphanage when I was a few days old, she left me with a birth certificate (I think). I was told the orphanage got flooded when I was two, and all documents had been destroyed. This, unfortunately, is a common line told to adoptees when they begin their search and are missing documents.

My adoptive parents arrived when I was about three years of

age—or so everyone assumed due to lack of good nutrition and physical care—but I must have been about five or six. A white woman was volunteering at the orphanage that all the children, including me, were transferred to after the destruction of the previous one. Unknowingly, at the time, the woman saw my "need" (according to her, I was in pretty bad shape) and determined she would "save me from the mud of Haiti's soil" via overseas adoption. In order to start the adoption process, I needed a birth certificate.

> *So, the people in the orphanage started searching, searching, and searching for something that would "work" for me. They came across a child's birth certificate who had passed away and never had a certificate of death.*

"Aha!" I can hear them saying, "this will do. The age looks about right. Who cares about the ridiculously long name and who cares that the mother on the birth certificate is not her actual mother. We need to make sure she claimed her daughter on her own and that there was no father involved. If she goes to search one day for her real family, she won't be able to really find them."

So there you have it. A year later, I sat in the adoptive parents' house with their one white biological child. I became the live dead girl. There are many issues and questions I have about this unethical adoption:

1. What happens if I search for the woman on my birth certificate? Will she think that her actual dead child is alive?

2. What happens if she wants a DNA test?

3. If I go to authorities now with this story, will I become a NOBODY?

4. Are there no records of my ACTUAL Birth Certificate with my real mother's ACTUAL name?

5. Now that I have my adoptive parent's last name (but not US Citizenship) does this mean that this dead person is really part

of them?

6. Who is this woman on the birth certificate? What was she like? Am I doing her justice?

7. How does this affect me wanting to emancipate myself from my adoptive family?

8. How does it affect my marriage?

9. How does it affect my daughter, who was adopted from Haiti too?

10. Am I supposed to be thankful that I am a dead girl who now has life?

Just until a few days ago, I actually thought that the mother on the birth certificate was actually my mother. Her last name was Cyr. I had known the "I was a dead girl" part, but I had thought that my birth certificate was just altered, meaning the rest of the information on it was true. It was not until I spoke with my biological brother that I realized that all of it is/was a lie and that the woman who supposedly "gave me up" was not even my mother!

Finding out that the little information I had is now nada makes me want to curl up in a ball, and roll back into the black hole I came from. It feels like I am left with nothing, and no hope. I can't answer the positive Whys of my life (e.g. why do I have a beautiful singing voice). And, I can't answer the negative Whys of my life (e.g. why do I feel sick every day. What is in my DNA that makes me ache?). I can't connect to anyone. I can't reach out.

Thankfully, my adoptive parents *did* make an effort to keep in contact with the lady who supposedly gave me up. We also sent her pictures of me when I was growing up. They stayed in contact with the orphanage, and we returned a couple of times to visit her, but I had no idea who she was. I just knew that after every visit, I returned home with a white lady and not the black lady. Did my biological mother know that the birth certificate they had for me was not mine? Did she even consider hers?

I am this dead person. If I attempt to

> *find my real birth certificate, can I become who I really am supposed to be? What's in a name? Power? Strength? Glory? Can I have peace if I never get my real birth certificate back?*

I want to meet my fake mother. I want to go back to Haiti and find the person on my birth certificate. Maybe I can be her daughter that died. Maybe I can live through her? Does she even know that her daughter died? Was her daughter put up for adoption and died of malnutrition?

Was this all some insane joke?

But, I also want my real birth certificate. I wanted pictures of me when I was a baby. I want to see my real mother's name on a document that belongs to ME, not someone else. Am I living my life to be the person she would have me be?

Has someone else taken my real Birth Certificate and become me? Does this make us? I don't want to be dead. I want to be more alive than ever. I want to be ME.

What's Been Trending

According to Dan Rather's 2014 report on AXS TV,[110] "Unwanted in America: The Shameful Side of International Adoption," adoption is currently a multi-billion dollar industry.

> *"Every year, American parents spend hundreds of millions of dollars on adopting children from abroad, money that goes straight to agencies. And they are the ones in charge of putting children in the hands of new parents. When you take a look at the numbers for international adoption, you'll discover that it is a global billion-dollar industry."*

Mr. Rather went on to reveal that 250,000 children have been adopted from China, Russia, India, Uganda, Congo, and Ethiopia. The report asked:

> *"Who is keeping track of these children?" The answer? A resounding: "No one."*

Adoptees of color made a statement on January 25, 2010, about what it means to be *saved* and *rescued* through adoption. "We uphold that Haitian children have a right to a family and a history that is their own and that Haitians themselves have a right to determine what happens to their own children. We resist the racist, colonialist mentality that positions the Western nuclear family as superior to other conceptions of family, and we seek to challenge those who abuse the phrase *Every child deserves a family* to rethink how this phrase is used to justify the removal of children from Haiti for the fulfillment of their own needs and desires. The desire for ownership of Haitian children directly contributes to the destruction of existing family and community structures in Haiti. This individualistic desire is supported by the historical and global anti-African sentiment which negates the validity of black mothers and fathers and condones the separation of black children from their families, cultures, and countries of origin."[111]

There seems to be a consensus that adoption is not the answer by assertive adoptees of color. "The best thing for orphans is to help reunite them with family members."[112] In the West, however, such an obvious answer has yet to be considered by those who have made and maintained international adoption laws, yet ignore protection of human rights.

Adoption agencies still flock to rural disaster zones and other troubled spots around the world. Young, single-parent families, who are considered illiterate or poverty-stricken or who have suffered displacement due to natural or human-made catastrophes, are the easiest targets for exploitation. One of the most striking examples of blatant adoption trafficking occurred after Haiti's 7.0 earthquake in 2010, which destroyed Port-au-Prince and killed more than 220,000 citizens.[113] A Baptist church member from Boise, Idaho, and leader of the "Haitian Orphan Rescue Mission" procured 33 children from a pastor at the Sharing Jesus Ministries. "Their plan was to scoop up 100 kids and take them by bus to a rented hotel at a beach resort in the Dominican Republic," where they planned to establish an orphanage. When asked for adoption papers for the children (and the problem of child trafficking), the group leader replied, "By no means are we any part of that. That is exactly what we are trying to combat."[114] The Haitian government, well aware of previous exploitation, sought to slow down these adoptions, fearing that the lack of proper paperwork would result in children being "forever separated from family members able and willing to care for them."[115] On the other hand, the church group planned to give the children to *loving Christian families*, so that each child could have *a new life in Christ*.

On the other hand, the Haitian residents have "mixed feelings toward Christian groups that funnel hundreds of millions into missions in Haiti."

Most deceptive to many of us orphans is that, in adoption law, the definition of the word *orphan* has been expanded to include children of unwed[116] and widowed mothers, leaving any child anywhere in the world at risk of being legally obtained for intercountry adoption (as long as the child's biological father did not legitimize the child, or the surviving parent has not remarried). It is easy to consider how agencies benefit when fathers are kept out of the picture as much as possible. The business of orphanages and adoption trafficking has become a serious global problem.

Paid child-finders and recruiters scout for the product to fill child care centers and orphanages. The trafficker will dupe naive parents from a country's rural areas, first dropping religious leaflets, or by gathering locals into small clusters and then preaching the benefits of letting their children go. They then register the children as *orphans* and then ship them to locations elsewhere in the country that are out of reach for the parents. The children do not return, and the parents continue to wait. As mentioned by Tinan Leroy, a contributor to *Adoptionland: From Orphans to Activists*, Haitian mothers have waited for decades. Arun Dohle, investigator and executive director of Against Child Trafficking (adopted from India to Germany 1970s), knows all too well that mothers, fathers, and siblings in Ethiopia, Malawi, and India (among others) still wait for reunions.

More than a few children have been abducted, manipulated, and recruited from the city streets of Africa, Asia, and Eastern

Europe, sold into orphanages, completely stripped of their identities, and given new documents. Investigative reports to that effect are published daily. Children are labeled, by way of adoption law, as *legal, paper, social,* or *manufactured* orphans, which gives the impression to Westerners (and, often, to the adopted person) that they have been orphaned by the death of both parents, abandoned, or that their extended families could not be found. When convincing parents to drop their rights, no one mentions a child market that expedites their removal and prevents them from returning to their families (even as adults).

Rather, the children are listed as *orphans, special needs, needy,* or *vulnerable* on adoption agency websites, and the applications pour in. It has been reported by adoptees and by journalists that the children in these ads are deprived of food, water, and other basic needs so that they will appear more deprived to tug at the heartstrings of potential adopters (and to create a sense of urgency). If the children are starving, let's remember that the parents are too. While the agencies are permitted to request tens-of-thousands of dollars per child, orphanage owners are given gifts and donations from Western buyers. Children are sent out to beg or to perform on the streets to attract donations from empathetic tourists. What is trending now? Religious volunteers who take *selfies* with the youngsters to prompt additional donations. This business is called *voluntourism,* and it is now rampant in developing nations.[117] More people realize that certain types of charitable help may do more harm than good, particularly when an inappropriate power relationship is formed between the giver and the receiver.

Many agencies have been known to reject the parents when they return for their children, as seen in the 2012 documentary *Mercy Mercy* by Katrine W. Kjaer. Anti-trafficking agreements, such as the United Nations Protocol to Prevent, Suppress, and Punish Trafficking in Persons, especially Women and Children, tend to ignore overseas adoption as involved with trafficking, despite the industry's prime targets: *women and children,* for fear of upsetting the rich consumer base. This neglect provides further protection for adoption traffickers. While all other traffickers search primarily for adults, prisoners, working-age men and women, and teenagers to put in forced labor, prostitution, and organ harvesting, adoption traffickers scour the land for the smallest among us: infants, babies, toddlers, and young children who are unable to speak for themselves, to remember, or to articulate their entrapment.

The United Nations Convention on the Rights of the Child should serve as preventative medicine against the problem of abduction, but profiteers have built a system that completely ignores child rights and routinely (and legally!) ships them around the globe. Adoption profiteers deny the pain and trauma inflicted upon the rejected families and, instead, focus on collecting fees, recruiting, harboring, deceiving, and transferring children for their *best interest,* all of which is officially, yet counter-intuitively, sanctioned.

Article 3, paragraph (a) of The United Nations Office of Drugs and Crime defines trafficking in persons as "the recruitment, transportation, transfer, harbouring, or receipt of persons, by means of threat or use of force or other forms of coercion, of abduction, of fraud, of deception, of the abuse of power or of a position of vulnerability or of the giving or receiving of payments or benefits to achieve the consent of a person having control over another person, for the purpose of exploitation. Exploitation shall include, at a minimum, the exploitation or the prostitution of others or other forms of sexual exploitation, forced labor or services, slavery or practices similar to slavery, servitude or the removal of organs."

Trafficking persons has three constituent elements: *the act (what is done)* recruitment, transportation, transfer, harboring (or receipt) of persons; *the means (how it is done),* threat or use of force, coercion, abduction, fraud, deception, abuse of power or vulnerability, or giving payments or benefits to a person in control of the victim; *the purpose (why it is done),* for the purpose of exploitation, including the prostitution of others, forced labor, the removal of organs, *and other types of exploitation.*

Against Child Trafficking has found

that mothers from Ethiopia (and other nations) are left only to pray for their children in the hope of finding solace.

Because of the industry polices itself, former orphans have had to investigate the industry on their own. For this reason, the evolution of the adoption industry needs to be scrutinized by those most affected: Previous "Orphans."

For this reason I am unable to promote or endorse any adoption agency or the child market for that matter, neither the industry as a whole—even under the Hague Adoption Convention—at this time. You will understand this position and why the treaty is referred to as the Hague *Abduction* Convention by the end of this book. During the most dire circumstances, we would encourage the parents' ability to successfully parent their own children and if the parents claimed they could not, another "positive" suggestion would be to uplift the family unit, next of kin, and so on and so forth. Avenues that would not alter the child's identity and permanently sever the child's ties to family.

Trained with a Teddy Bear

In an endeavor to clean up the perception that the industry is toxic, the adoption lobby created a strategy to give the impression that African mothers are making an *informed choice*. In one particular demonstration, educators used a teddy bear as a physical teaching tool to guide mothers (Haitians, in this particular scenario) about how to relinquish their children using the so-called legal and thus ethical *informed choice*.[118] Since many Westerners no longer buy into the shaming and blaming, the training methods have expanded farther afield. I was shocked to learn that African women receive the same counseling today that was used sixty years ago in the Americas, Europe, and Asia.

An educational training video can be found online disclosing how the Haitian people are currently being groomed to *legally* abandon babies for approved trade. Instead of adoption as a last resort, parents can directly relinquish their children for intercountry adoption, just like in privileged Western nations. Moreover, little other help, or options, are offered to the people on the African continent.

At first glance, *informed consent* appears ethical. However, after watching a video about the evolution of adoption education, one can pinpoint the deception hidden below the surface. The video illustrates how the pro-adoption campaign plants the seed to relinquish children in the minds of an uninformed community (as if it were a fair solution).[119]

The counselor explains that a full adoption means that "all bonds between child and parents will be cut" and that "every intercountry adoption is a full adoption." Conversely, the lecture works akin to hypnotic suggestion with families who would normally never consider such an extreme measure are implanted with the idea instead of turning to local, less severe, less invasive, and less traumatic solutions such as kinship, temporary, or community care to keep the family unit together. Those without an agenda (or not under the influence of agency rhetoric) would, instinctively, advocate for the rights of families and communities. However, the function of adoption training (at least to the intuitive observer) results in additional protection *for the agency*, which can then claim that it briefed the mother, but she still chose to give *informed consent*. It deceptively leads the local community and authorities to believe that sending children overseas benefits everyone involved (while completely ignoring the painful long-term consequences). Overseas adoption permanently disrupts the lives of the people it leaves behind.

A trainer introduces herself to a student group and starts the program by saying: "I want the best for my child."

The camera zooms in on her, a professionally-dressed Haitian woman, holding a small stuffed bear serving as the infant in the relinquishment demonstration. "And then you pass it on," she says, turning to a younger woman standing at the front of the class.

The young woman faces her classmates and copies the phrase, "I want the best for my child. So I free it for adoption." She passes the bear to another female student at the informational session. Even the elder men are duped into accepting this Western concept of *child protection*.

The next person to hold the bear repeats the statement: "I give my child for adoption because I want the best for my child." She looks to the instructor, for what appears to be approval, before passing the bear to the next student.

A tall, thin woman approaches the front of the class. She introduces herself and repeats the phrase: "I want the best for my child." After delivering her endorsement, she also turns to the instructor for approval.

Another professional explains, "We [Haitians] want the best

for our child. That is the most important to us."

In the latest educational training, the instructor informs the class that no more contact with the child is allowed. "No exchange. You get no address, no phone number, no name, no Facebook contact. Nothing."

She goes on to explain that, "The child must settle in its new family. Any dialogue with the Haitian family would only disturb the children. It would be difficult for the child if the Haitian family tried to connect."

She concludes the talk, reminding the students: "Don't forget, all we do is for the well-being of the child."

Unknown to these Haitian citizens, the fact that the agency set up a child processing shop in their territory should be considered a violation against the rights of their families and their children. The very presence of lucrative adoption agencies in charge of *child welfare* and *protection* inside a foreign territory sabotages less destructive, less severe solutions from being offered to the land's people. The most disturbing tactic of the industry is the lies disseminated in the West, accusing the mother of abandoning the child. The reality is that the mother was *trained* to surrender her rights in the most civilized of manners. Then the immediate removal of the child at the expense of the mother and the community's reputation makes her appear heartless as if she never *wanted* the child in the first place. Furthermore, the destination country has no say regarding the deprived mother. She has no way to defend herself or to explain her side of the story. The adoption industry makes inexperienced parents believe that they are inadequate. At the same time, their children grow up, believing that they were *abandoned.*

The instructor continues to steadfastly cajole the mother into thinking about relinquishment as if her love is not enough. The counseling convinces mothers to assume that they do not have what it takes for their child to do well. "We must think about that [relinquishment] very well, because we, most of all, want our child to do well."

Receptive African students listen and learn. One young Haitian woman studies what appears to be a script. Another Haitian woman stares at the floor while rocking back and forth.

In the end, the students look down as the instructor paints every adoption in a positive light, as *gifts* for more deserving couples or a "better" life. This particular indigenous community was told, "Most important is that you decide with your heart in the interest of the child. While you know it [adoption] is the best for the child; it is about the well-being of the child, and you have to be convinced." Again, reiterating a fear that their care and love was not their child's best interest.

Because of the constant demand for adoptable babies by citizens of Western superpowers, the pressure groups must keep the flood-gates open for *available* children. Today, facilitators vie for the Hague "stamp of approval" to color their businesses as ethical.

This type of counseling empowers the industry, protects the global market, and infringes upon the rights and abilities of parents from native communities. *Letting children go,* especially hurts families and parents when they become elderly and rely on their grown children for social security, retirement care, and welfare. With their adult children forever gone and without any recourse, the elderly parents without their children often have little other support.

If an exploited mother ever said she did not know the full meaning of adoption, the industry can counter that she received counseling before she made her decision.

> *However, for those of us adopted, we wonder, Is this not the wrong kind of counseling?*

(Sounded more like *convincing* or *coercing* than counseling to those of us who have witnessed it first-hand.)

Mae Claire's situation represents just one of thousands of private conversations adults (adopted as children) have been having with each other about how adoption has displaced them. When people argue against the practice, facilitators stubbornly push more fiercely for positive stories in an attempt to save face, claiming that the children have been sent to *better homes*, based solely on the financial and material wealth of their clients. The adopted person is snagged somewhere in the middle. However, what matters most to the parents is the fact that they are deprived of their children and unable to have any contact (even after they become adults).

Still Trending

To the horror of those who know better (and are well-informed about agency tactics), rural African mothers are now losing children at alarming rates *as if it serves them*. The system purports to provide relief to poor parents but does nothing to uplift or to empower them. Instead, agencies earn income from convincing mothers to relinquish their children. When the mothers experience pain and turmoil, the facilitators, lobbyists, and profiteers turn against them, and those who represent the victim. These parents are forced to cope with their private devastation, left to believe that they will receive correspondence from the Western adopters, but usually end up dying years later after receiving (maybe) one or two letters (if they are lucky). Such grief can lead to more than a few parents to commit suicide. Seeing their African children being adored by American (or other Western) guardians, these mothers are left with the impression that the Western couples are concerned about African welfare and, therefore, might even send the family funds after the adoptive parents have obtained the child(ren) for adoption. These African parents are often groomed for the brief farewell parties where they will see their children for the last time. The prospective couples convince the parents that they are friendly and trustworthy, and will send letters and photos regularly and that they care about the adopted child(ren)'s family. Both parties are unaware of the psychology and emotional trauma that can occur because of the separation. Letters may be sent during the honeymoon phase of adoption, but eventually, these feelings of goodwill can fade away as the adopters become more secure and intent in the idea that the children of color really do *belong* to them. Suddenly, ties to the child(ren)'s family can be cut, and the unquestioning African mothers, such as the ones currently being groomed in Ethiopia, Uganda, Haiti, Nigeria, and Kenya (just to name a few of the targeted hot spots) are not warned of the lasting confusion that many transracially- and intercountry-adopted children experience throughout their lifetimes, such as why they "were not good enough to be kept" or the assumption that they were *abandoned*.

Documentaries, such as *Mercy Mercy,* show Ethiopian parents being threatened by the owners of agencies then left powerless to fight against an industry that has only caused them grief. It has become a standard practice to suggest intercountry adoption for parents who have chronic diseases by charities training in other countries to provide *ethical* child protection measures. These parents mourn their missing children, and the "unknowing" of their status makes it that much more excruciating. The lack of support for victims of adoption trafficking and the acute need for Western legislation to protect families against agency practices is the most troubling. Child trafficking laws need to be set up in the West that will hold these agencies accountable. If this is not accomplished, these families and future families will continue to be victimized by the adoption industry in the near and far future.

Message from a Real Ethiopian Orphan

"As I live my life, I do what I do because she has left that part of herself to me. She fought the fight of freedom and never gave up, and I will continue that tradition too, for as long as I live."

~Roman Akafate, a previous orphan[120]

Roman Akafate, a former shepherd girl from a rural African village and a *real orphan*, and not a manufactured one created by the adoption industry, is now a mother of four daughters living in the United States. Roman was born and raised by a single mother named Zenebech Biru, in Addis Ababa, Ethiopia, in East Africa. Ethiopian citizens, like Roman, are proud to be the only African nation that has never been colonized. For this, there is much delight among its citizenry.

Roman remembers her mother as a strong, nurturing, and hardworking woman. She "raised all seven of us without any help from the men who fathered us." Zenebech owned a small coffee house, an impressive feat for a woman in 1960s Ethiopia "with no educational backgrounds."

At only five-years-old, life for Roman seemed secure, and her mother's business blossomed. Devastatingly, this confident woman became infected with food poisoning and, within days of being admitted to the hospital, died. Her untimely death left seven children orphaned.

To add to the family's tragedy, Roman's eldest brother, newly coping with the trauma, wracked with grief over their mother's death, and overwhelmed from caring for his six younger siblings, passed away suddenly (at the age of fourteen) from kidney failure within two months of their mother's passing.

Little Roman and her five siblings, all under the age of ten, were dispersed among extended family members to separate homes and villages. Roman was sent to live with her "great-grandpa," an eighty-year-old man, named Amosha Akafate, who lived in a remote Ethiopian territory. Roman points out that the land was devoid of modern-day luxuries, such as electricity, tap water, phones, and vehicles. When she first arrived, the neighboring children were curious about her shoes (as something so essential was considered a luxury).[121]

Her great-grandfather sometimes retrieved water from the springs or rivers and, at times, traversed long distances barefoot to collect firewood for cooking their meals over an open fire. Compared to the busy life she had with her mother and siblings, the isolated environment was unfamiliar to five-year-old Roman. "Though," she writes, "I soon got used to it and adjusted myself to this way of life."

Because they lived with farm animals, her great-grandfather's house might have been infected by fleas or other parasites, they fell ill to scabies and other illnesses, but the wistful memories with the grand man were, "probably the happiest days I had since my mom passed away."

Today, Roman still appreciates nostalgic memories of "sitting together" with her great grandfather while "watching the cattle graze and drink[ing] water from the nearby spring."

Living in a simple rural environment gave her the ability to "enjoy all of God's creations in their pure and natural forms without too much manipulation." She believes they were experiencing green living [before it became a fad among the elite]. Because of the isolation, she "enjoyed striking sunrises and sunsets, but the moon and stars that lit up the night were the icings on the cake." Moreover, Roman asserts that such an environment "was as close to God as one could ever be." She feels blessed to be the one chosen to live in such a landscape and so "in touch with nature and all the living things that make our world as wonderful as it is."

Roman gives credit and thanks to her great-grandfather for the spirit and determination she now has as a woman living in the United States. "If I had not had his love and support when I needed it most and especially because we did not have much (only love), I was able to make the best of things when I needed to have an optimistic outlook on life." She was never adopted but rather moved around to various family members and communities while she was growing up.

Could time with her great-grandfather, eighty years-of-age, have occurred if adoption agencies were there to second-guess his judgment?

In 2014, Roman listened to a conference call organized by the Joint Council on International Children Services (JCICS), a self-proclaimed child advocacy organization with partners in fifty-two countries. The JCICS served as the advisory board for the Council of Accreditation (COA), where adoption agencies go to get accredited. The JCICS proudly reaped the benefits of "sitting on the seat of three coalitions which influence programs and spending representing billions of dollars for children living outside of family care and children adopted both domestically and internationally."

The purpose of the teleconference was to ultimately "come up with a plan" to remedy what these top administrators perceived to be a *toxic* situation, one with *no advancement*. Their biggest fear was that they would be demonized as traffickers.[122] Surely they would do whatever it took to legalize their work and to present that work in the best of light.

About twenty-five heads, of high-grossing adoption agencies, discussed the obstacles that prevented them from obtaining the rights to children for overseas shipment, despite a large staff and "a lot of advocacy." The obstacles included parents not showing up or a television show presenting adoption in a negative light. The group discussed possible ways to overcome the roadblocks, such as better agency tactics, and gaining the trust and attention of Ethiopian citizens through the use of various mass marketing media enlisting the help of their adoptive parents worldwide.

"It's become toxic," stated one leader to his peers during the teleconference. He feared that the public would rise up and convince themselves that he was a demon and that his work should be stopped. He hoped to lobby the government. "If we don't do something in the public forum, to counter the demonization, there could be a complete stoppage and no real future."

Adoption agencies strategically choose positive Christian based words to gain a following (*God, love, hope, faith, save, trust, children, home, forever family*, and *heart*) in order to reinforce the associations in their charitable child-centric names and subsequent campaigns. Another representative from a cleverly-named agency preferred public appeals instead of advocating directly with the government since they had been doing that for years. She showed them the centralized authorities in China and the US as examples of what she was trying to accomplish. She worried that the African public was receptive yet, "they don't change to allow for more adoptions." She believed "the caucus must be really strategic."

> *For years, industry insiders have used the most heartbreaking black-and-white images of children to drive donations, convincing trusting prospective couples to apply for a child. It makes sense that whenever they presented children alone, in black and white, or climbing a garbage heap, the funds and non-refundable applications poured in.*

Western white adopters were among the most helpful marketers. They sent home videos of happy Ethiopian children in American homes to counter any objection to adoption, in general, by presenting these images and stories of *good* adoptions to smother out any attention to the abuse, including the recent death of Hana Alemu Befekadu Williams (1997–2011), an Ethiopian girl murdered by her evangelical adopters. These devout American Christians used a fundamentalist parenting training manual, called *How to Train Up a Child*, to force the little girl to abide by the rules of their household. The author advised parents to whip children with skinny tree branches, to hit them with PVC pipes, to punish them with cold-water baths, and to hose them off if they had potty training accidents (as these types of punishments left no marks and, thus, would not alert the authorities). The theme of the book was to discipline a child until it is "without breath to complain."[123]

In the United States since 2009, Ethiopia has been the second most popular nation for Americans to adopt from, after China and before Russia. Between 1999 and 2015, facilitators sent 15,135 Ethiopian children to the U.S.[124] Roman has listened to narratives from several online adoptee rights groups, has been particularly empathetic to Korean-born adoptees, and she did not want the same thing to happen to the children of her homeland. To that end, she wrote a public plea to The Ethiopian Government officials and to the national media. Here is a portion of her letter:

"I am not a politician by any stretch of the imagination, but I have a deep concern of my own about what has been happening to Ethiopian innocent children and their poor families. As you might have known, children have been sent to foreign countries to foreign people's houses all over the world all in the name of adoption.

This cruel practice of selling children in the name of adoption has been expanded all over Ethiopian provinces, and tens of thousands of children have been bought and sold right on the open market but under a disguised name called intercountry adoption.

We had witnessed some cruelty and abuses some of the adopted Ethiopian children were and still are suffering in the hands of their adopting families. There is a lot that is going on that I will not go into right now . . . .

The result they are looking for is to successfully have access to the children they can then sell to foreigners who are willing and able to pay them as much as tens of thousands of dollars per child. They have sold so many of our children for years and years, and now there is a temporary stop to the adoption process that has them in panic. To these agencies, Ethiopian children are just transactions with tens of thousands of dollars per head. They are desperate beyond belief and shamefully discussing their desperate plans on how they could play the government, the media, and Ethiopian parents.

They discuss not only about having their hands on real orphans but also on those children who have live parents. It is really sickening hearing their discussion, but I am glad they are exposed. I am glad they, themselves have told the truth of the matter, that they are in it to win it and win it big time by having the government open the temporarily closed doors."

Voices like Roman's are typically dismissed. To allow *orphans* and their allies to speak so openly infuriates those who perpetuate the lies. Roman, a mother herself, knows it is impossible to compete against corporate giants, but her support is invaluable to adoptees, especially when it comes to protecting the future lives of children and their families. The COA has since folded, on March 6, 2014, and the Joint Council for International Children Services threw in the towel, effective June 30, 2015,[125] after forty years of *serving the world's children*. The board claimed they were subjected to "the same trends that have impacted many of our partners over the last decade." The board chair, an adopter who benefitted from the organization, also admitted this: "We are simply out of money," in his outgoing email.[126]

Like many of us, Roman is an advocate for the right for children to remain with their families and not to be exploited for intercountry adoption. Roman concludes that the years she spent as a little shepherd girl with her great-grandfather was the best time of her life. "Everything was perfectly wonderful until that point." Her life became brighter during those years, and by the memories she has of them.

Wisdom gained from experiences like hers provide evidence that *poverty-stricken* children do not have to be taken out of their *dire* situations, or nations of birth, to be happy. Well-being is found by adapting to one's circumstances and becoming empowered in the process. The ability to stay with family and within a community keeps a child safe and secure into adulthood.

*Ethiopia reportedly suspended intercountry adoption in November of 2017 and banned the practice as of February 2018 according to the country's state-run News Agency ENA, citing it made children "vulnerable to identity crisis, psychological problems, and violation of rights."[127]

PART 5: WALK IN AWARENESS

Walkabout

"I belong to this land, and the land belongs to me."

~Doris Garimara Pilkington (July 1, 1937 - April 10th, 2014)
Australian Aborigine and author of *Rabbit Proof Fence*

Australian Aboriginals

Between 1910 and 1970, the Australian government officials removed up to 100,000 Aboriginal children (most of whom were under the age of five) from their biological families.[128] The authorities intended to protect the children from their inferior native heritage and to assimilate them into *civilized* society. As a consequence, many of the Aboriginal children sent to church boarding schools, state institutions, and foster or adoptive homes suffered physical and sexual abuse. Today, this population is called the "Stolen Generation."[129]

Most children were extracted to *save* them from what the Australian officials presumed to be the parents' inability to raise their children. Some of these Australian Aboriginal adoptees fought the emotional battle to reunite with their tribal communities. Many questioned their forced adoptions by a government that saw their mothers as *wretched people*. Some of their stories have been heard in Australia's mainstream media.

Authorities had previously kept the public from knowing about the practice, and as a result, the extraction of children was typically hailed as a *win-win for all.*

In 1941, Doris Pilkington Garimara, at the age of three-and-a-half, was taken from her Aboriginal mother to live at the Moore River Mission. She was told that she had been abandoned while she was growing up. At the age of twenty-five, she was able to find her mother. The elderly woman broke down, revealing, "I did not give you away. The government took you away. And it hurt me so much to leave you."[130]

Ten years after their reunion, Doris finally heard her mother's version of the story. Far from being abandoned, Doris learned that she was forcibly separated as part of an official government program. Children were removed under ministerial warrants, and their mothers had no say in the matter. Life separated from her mother, coupled with a strict Christian upbringing, caused Doris to believe that her people and their practices involved devil worship and evil doing. "I was very frightened," she said in an article published in *The Sydney Morning Herald*, "because the Christian [...] brainwashing [...] was still there and I had to undo that before I would learn anything about my own culture, language, ethnic history, where my people came from, and who they were." It was only after listening to her mother's side of the story that Doris decided to learn more about her indigenous culture.

After this journey of self-discovery, Doris's opinion about her own culture changed. She admitted that, for a long time, "I was angry, particularly at the missionaries who brought me up to believe the Aboriginal people were dirty and evil." It took her ten years to say, "I belong to this land, and the land belongs to me." Doris shared that her reunion with her mother, and the return trip to her country, was pivotal for her own healing. Able to learn her language with the hope of being able to speak with some of the older people, she considered herself one of the lucky ones. Since learning the truth about her mother, she has written four books documenting three generations of women in her family.

In 1996, Doris released a book based on her Aboriginal

mother's trek, called *Follow the Rabbit Proof Fence,* and published by the University of Queensland Press. The narrative featured Molly Kelly (1917-2004) named Molly Craig at birth, Doris's Aboriginal mother. In 1931, Molly (aged fourteen) and her younger sister, Daisy Burungu, and their cousin, Gracie Fields, ages ten and six, were taken from their home by Australian authorities and sent to live far from the tribe. Unable to adjust to the *better* life at the religious boarding school without their mothers, they defied the authorities and escaped. Molly Kelly led the two younger girls using instincts to guide her. For nine weeks and over 1,600 kilometers (roughly 1,000 miles) through the harsh desert, they followed a rabbit fence to guide them from the Moore River Settlement to their home in Jigalong. Their journey is still considered "one of the most remarkable feats of endurance, cleverness, and courage in Australian history." The 2002 screenplay, *Rabbit Proof Fence,* based on Doris's book, brought the issues to a larger audience. The movie added a visual dimension, as viewers see through the eyes of the Aboriginal girls, making for a believable and necessary interior point of view.

A public servant in Western Australia and prime bureaucrat responsible for the government policy, the Chief Protector of Aborigines (who was born in Northumberland, England), called the film a "gross distortion of the truth." His son, John Neville, told *The Sydney Sun-Herald* that his father sought to "help half-castes who faced hostility from both sides: Aborigines and the whites," and that his father "had great respect for full-blood Aborigines. He wanted to help them become civilised."[131] According to adult adopted people of all races and creeds, this attitude of superiority, often referred to as the savior complex, continues to this day.[132]

Doris's younger sister, also taken by authorities sixty years prior and raised to believe that she was orphaned, chose not to acknowledge her Aboriginal roots, and did not express interest in reuniting with their mother. The loss was painful for the Aboriginal heroine of *Follow the Rabbit Proof Fence.* Her biggest regret was never reuniting with her younger daughter. Molly Kelly died in 2004 in her sleep at the age of 87.[133] Doris died of ovarian cancer a decade later at the age of 76.[134]

Perspectives from the Stolen Generations

Comments made by Aboriginal adoptees on the *Bringing Them Home* report,[135] match comments made worldwide by adopted people and throughout history. Submission 617 reported a typical international adoptee's confusion, yet it was a contribution from an Aboriginal woman, "Most of us girls were thinking white in the head but were feeling black inside. We weren't black or white. We were a very lonely, lost, and sad displaced group of people. We were taught to think and act like a white person, but we didn't know how to think and act like an Aborigine. We didn't know anything about our culture. We were completely brainwashed to think only like a white person. As we grew into adults and began mixing into the mainstream society, we found we were not accepted [because] we were Aboriginal. When we went and mixed with Aborigines, some found we couldn't identify with them either, because we had too much white ways in us. So we were neither black or white. We were simply a lost generation of children. I know. I was one of them."

Adopted people are still fighting the same private battle as the Aboriginal adoptees of yesteryear. Both the Australian government and adoption facilitators believed they were taking the *right* actions based on their misinformed belief systems. The extraction was meant to *save* children from (what the organization assumed to be) a parent's inability to raise them and then to assimilate the children into *better, new,* or *improved* environments.

* * *

Similarities between Aboriginal adoptees and current international adoptees include:
- Taken miles away from any family connection.
- Issued a new identity.
- Prevented from speaking their mother tongue.
- Made to feel ashamed for wanting to know more about

their origins.
• Discouraged against finding their families.

The mainstream society was led to believe that:
• The children were orphans.
• Mothers routinely abandon their children.
• Birthplace and culture were *wrong* and *inferior* to the *new* and *better* adoptive family and culture.
•Displacement was *for God, of God,* and therefore child protection also deemed *in the child's best interest.* As a consequence, the transaction was not questioned.

Reintegration was sabotaged by:
• Communication was nearly impossible during a reunion; therefore, family reconciliation was discouraged due to the lack of common language.
• The facilitator did little to connect or repair communication between the separated family members.
• The facilitator refused to admit any wrong-doing or trauma inflicted upon the families, but rather blamed the victims.
• Even as adults, the displaced children were not legally permitted to contact or locate their families, or have any follow up at all.

In submission 338, Victoria, stated:

> *"Our life pattern was created by the government policies and are forever with me, as though an invisible anchor around my neck. The moments that should be shared and rejoiced by a family unit, for [my brother] and mum and I are forever lost. The stolen years that are worth more than any treasure are irrecoverable."*

A South Australian man, removed from his home in the

1950s at age seven, reported that the "[adoptive family] started to get very nasty towards me. Every time I would sit down at the table for meals [they] would always have something to say to me: about my manners at the table, how to sit, how to chew, how to eat, when to eat. If I would make a mistake they would pull my hair bending my head until it hurt. I would cry saying sorry. I couldn't understand them. It seemed like I was always in the wrong. I started to feel very uncomfortable. I kept crying and thinking about my family. I wanted to go home. I was sick and tired of this sort of life. I hated it. I was very upset with this family. I couldn't even see anybody to tell them what was happening. A lady from the welfare came to see me. I told her how I was feeling. She just took no notice of me and done her reports saying I was very happy with [them]. I just had to put up with it all. So one day I went to Port Adelaide and stole a pocket knife from one of the stores just so I could get into trouble and leave this family."[136]

A woman from New South Wales removed to a girls' home in Parramatta at the age of thirteen, and subsequently placed in domestic service in the 1960s, had this to say, "The thing that hurts the most is that they didn't care about who they put us with. As long as it looked like they were doing their job, it just didn't matter."[137]

The First to Win Compensation:

Australia's "National Sorry Day"[138] is an annual event (started in 1998 and commemorated on May 26th) to remember the Stolen Generations from the Aboriginal and Torres Strait Islander communities. Removed from his home as a child on false information, Bruce Trevorrow[139] became the first of Australia's Stolen Generations to win compensation. In 1957, Bruce's Aboriginal parents asked their neighbors, Mr. And Mrs. Evans, to take their thirteen-month son to a hospital 150 kilometers away (as the Evans's were the only people in the area with a car).

The hospital admittance record described the boy as a *neglected child without parents* suffering from malnutrition and infective diarrhea. The intake sheet falsely stated, "the mother has cleared out and the father is boozing" and claimed that the father was "nourishing the children with alcohol." After a visit to the household in 1957, a newly-hired staff member from the Aborigine Protection Board drafted a letter stating that Bruce's father was illiterate, unemployed, and a *habitual drunkard*. Despite the fact that Bruce's parents were married, the children were classified as *illegitimate*.

Because Bruce's parents did not have a phone (or a car), they wrote to the hospital to inquire about their son and asked when he might be released. Twelve days after his admission, Bruce was discharged from the hospital and into the care of a white foster family by a welfare officer from the South Australian Aborigines Department. The hospital had already sent him to a couple who responded to a newspaper advertisement in their quest to become *parents*. The couple was told that he was neglected and abandoned because his mother had "gone on a walkabout." Without having to complete all the paperwork involved, the couple was approved by the Aborigines Protection Board to take Bruce. The unrelated woman was given custody before she was even licensed to care for anyone.

Bruce's mother wrote a letter asking for permission to retrieve him, "How long before I can have him home as I have not forgot I got a baby in there." She ended the request, stating, "I trust you will let me know as soon as possible" and signed off with, "Yours faithfully," suggesting an (unfounded) assurance in the system.

However, the welfare officer lied, claiming the boy was "making good progress" and that the doctor had not yet approved him for release. Truthfully, she had already sent Bruce to someone else.

During another attempt by his mother to learn of Bruce's status, the welfare worker refused to agree to release the boy, making the determination that the woman's home was "not in any way satisfactory" and wrote in a report that she was living *improperly* with Joseph (Bruce's father) for years. The employee also accused her of being "a most unsuitable mother for any of her children."

By the age of three, Bruce had developed psychological problems, including a condition known as trichotillomania, in which infants pull out clumps of hair. He was diagnosed as depressed, developed a speech defect, chewed his clothing, damaged books, and stole.

> *Child psychologists and psychiatrists persuaded the judge that, based on the chronology of the events, the little boy's problems were "caused by the maternal deprivation he suffered by being removed from his natural mother."*

In the adoptive home, Bruce knew he was not the couple's child. The woman claimed that he was really white, but darker-skinned due to distant relatives. She eventually became sick and threatened to force him to "leave the family and be placed elsewhere." When Bruce's behavior became too much for her, she returned him. He told the court that he was shocked when he met his mother because he believed she would be white.[140]

November of 1966 and on his tenth birthday, Bruce was reunited with his mother, under supervision. Bruce's father had, unfortunately, passed away that year.

Mr. Burnside, a barrister for the high court representing Trevorrow, stated: "The fact is he had grown up to the age of nine with a completely false identity, an identity that was not his, an identity about which he was misled."

Bruce Trevorrow became the first Aborigine to win compensation after launching legal action against the South Australian government. Removal from his family had had a domino effect on his life, leading to many problems, even as an older adult. Because his Aboriginal siblings went on to live successful lives with their parents, Bruce could compare his experience against theirs. The harmful consequences of being taken from his family were evident. He was awarded $450,000 for injuries and losses suffered and a further $75,000 in damages for unlawful removal and false imprisonment. All in all, he grieved over a "loss of identity, depression, alcoholism, and erratic employment."

The Australian reported that Mr. Trevorrow was awarded $550,000 in damages and $225,000 in interest the year he had passed away.[141] Justice Gray's central finding was that Bruce "suffered seriously from his childhood separation. It clearly exacerbated his existing physical disabilities."

In 2007, *The Age* reported Trevorrow encouraging other members of The Stolen Generation to take court action.

"Just keep on going, "

he said after his win. He had a relationship with two brothers by birth who were well-respected within their Njarrindjeri community and could provide support.

In response, the South Australian Government lodged an appeal against Justice Gray's decision in February 2008. In June of that same year, Bruce Trevorrow died of a heart attack. He was fifty-one.

* * *

Children have been taken unethically from families globally and throughout history. The good news has been the adopted person's ability to connect and to communicate with anyone anywhere due to the worldwide web. We can caution humanity about the hidden side of adoption so that future generations will not have to bear the same, unnecessary pain. From a historical view, humanity is better able to protect and empower itself now. The hope is that the mainstream society will acknowledge the value of the tribe and of our ancestral blood-ties. In an effort to see the grand scheme of things, this book is meant to be a rallying cry for us to do everything in our power to stop remove price tags from children, worldwide, once and for all.[142]

Apologies

From the 1930s to the early 1980s, the White Stolen Generations represent an estimated 250,000 Australian–born non-indigenous children removed from their families for what was claimed to be another *positive* practice for mothers and children.

One of these mothers, Christine Cole, is quoted as saying,

> *"I had my baby taken from me in 1969, and I think the use of the term forced adoption polarises the actual phenomena of what was going on. What was going on was kidnapping children, kidnapping newborn babies from their mothers at birth."*

She went on to say,

"We certainly need a central database because there are many adoptees who are undocumented, so they just turned up as if they sort of landed here from some alien place." [143]

* * *

On February 13, 2008, Kevin Rudd, the Australian Prime

Minister, delivered an apology to the Australian Aborigines and to the Stolen Generations in what is now referred to as Australia's Sorry Day.[144] The following is an excerpt from the apology: "To say to you, the Forgotten Australians, and those who were sent to our shores as children without your consent, we are sorry... Sorry that as children you were taken from your families and placed in institutions where so often you were abused. [...] As a nation, we must now reflect on those who did not receive proper care. We look back with shame that many of you were left cold, hungry and alone and with nowhere to hide and nobody to whom to turn.[145]"

Since that 2008 apology, mothers have pushed for an apology for what they call "kidnappings," also known as "forced adoptions."

Two years later, on February 24, 2010, former Prime Minister of the United Kingdom, Gordon Brown, publically apologized on behalf of Britain's role in similar schemes. Documentaries report as many as 500,000 were children sent to orphanages, boarding schools, and other institutions.[146]

More than a few of the grieving victims declared that the apology was "too little, too late." The children, now elderly, had to cope with their emotional wounds for their entire lives. One man, tearful and distressed, told Margaret Humphreys, a Nottingham social worker, "I'm almost seventy-five years old. I've never been home, but I'm still British. I've been [in Australia] more than sixty years."[147] Additionally, at least one survivor stated that they'd rather see the church charities make an apology since the forced emigration had been initiated and pushed through by the religious clergy under the pretext of *Godly* morals and dogmatic ideals. Despite the lost time, words from these survivors live on, serving as a beacon of light for the younger victims of the Baby Scoop Era and the Baby Swoop Generations, who are nearing, or well beyond middle-age, transported from one territory to another on the assumption that these placements were *for [their] best interest.*

At the Great Hall in Canberra, Julia Gillard, Australia's 27th

Prime Minister, delivered a national apology[148] for the "forced adoption practice" that occurred between the 1950s and the 1970s.[149] More than 800 people were in attendance. The following is an excerpt from (Australia's) *ABC News*, March 21, 2013:

"Today, this Parliament, on behalf of the Australian people, takes responsibility and apologises for the policies and practices that forced the separation of mothers from their babies which created a lifelong legacy of pain and suffering,"

"We acknowledge the profound effects of these policies and practices on fathers and we recognise the hurt these actions caused to brothers and sisters, grandparents, partners and extended family members.

We deplore the shameful practices that denied you, the mothers, your fundamental rights and responsibilities to love and care for your children.

You were not legally or socially acknowledged as their mothers and you yourselves were deprived of care and support.

You were given false assurances. You were forced to endure the coercion and brutality of practices that were unethical, dishonest and in many cases illegal."

The crowd erupted with applause and many broke down in tears at several points throughout the speech. Ms. Gillard acknowledged that despite the apology, victims will still suffer.

"Friends, as the time for birth came, these babies would be snatched away before they had even held them in their arms,"

Sometimes, consent was achieved by forgery or fraud. Sometimes women signed adoption papers whilst under the influence of medication.

Most common of all was the bullying arrogance of a society that presumed to know what was best.

The hurt did not simply last for a few days or weeks. This was a wound that would not heal."

Gillard also acknowledged children who suffered sexual abuse at the hands of their adopters or in institutions.

> *On March 21, 2013, Australia's 28th Prime Minister, Tony Abbott, restated the apology, admitting that he could not "imagine a grief greater than that of a parent and a child parted from each other" nor "an ache greater than the fear that mum didn't want me, especially since it wasn't true. "*

Despite these apologies, adoption is still considered a form of *child protection* and *in the child's best interest* in the white-collar political and mainstream landscape. As a result, mothers, like Marineta Ciofu in Romania, still wait and grieve for their daughters and sons. And Korean fathers, like the one who flagged for my attention in a back alley, still search and wonder. Furthermore, every day, countless children are matched with foreigners and shipped all over the world as if empty vessels easily given a new identity. Australian mothers received an apology. Canadian mothers initiated an inquiry. American mothers are organizing. Will mothers from Asia and Africa soon join the fight? Only time will tell.

About Rev. Dr. Janine Myung Ja

Rev. Dr. Janine Myung Ja has produced numerous books and works, ranging from anthologies, history, philosophy, and personal. She works to bring the crisis of adoption trafficking to public awareness and is an advocate of the investigational field research and reports from Against Child Trafficking (ACT). Janine believes that every angle of adoption needs to be acknowledged—especially the unknown side, which consists of the entire landscape. Did you know only ten states out of fifty allow unrestricted access to adoptees born within the US?

In 2011, Janine and her twin initiated a group on social media called Adoption Truth and Transparency Worldwide Information Network (ATTWIN). The diverse community consists of domestic, late-discovery, transracial and international adoptees and family members within the United States and overseas who had been separated by adoption.

Since learning that children are abducted and overseas under the veneer of love and charity, the mission of ACT USA has been to inform and educate the public on the crisis of an unknown type of trafficking, which solely focuses on children. One such event is an upcoming Adoption Trafficking Awareness Symposium.

Janine appreciates the voices of those who are willing to look deeper into the adoption landscape and invites adopted people to join ATTWIN for discussion. Unlike entities that profit from the child market, ATTWIN advocates for equal rights for all humans. Antiquated adoption laws disregard innate human rights that are enshrined in the US Constitution AND the United Nations Convention on the Rights of the Child (UNCRC).

NOTE FROM THE RESEARCHER

Hi! And thanks for reading! This book is one of a series I call "Rare Adoption Books for Adults." The reason I've named it as such is because most adoption books you'll find are written by adoptive parents for children in an attempt to help them adapt to the adoptive family. However, after participating in the *adult* adoptee community for more than twenty-five years, I've learned that there are numerous additional burdens that we are forced to contend with. And these concerns have yet to be acknowledged among the mainstream. Fortunately, more and more adopted people are finding their way to resources and information and I'm happy to have been part of that even though it's been a very long and lonely journey consisting of isolated research and self doubt. If you found value in any part of the content of this book, I'd love it if you would leave a comment in the review section of the book's profile at the online retailer. And, if you would leave a few comments on the book's profile, I'd be especially appreciative. Hope we meet through books again!

Janine

PS For stories from adopted people all over the world, consider picking up *Adoptionland: From Orphans to Activists* or *Adoption Stories: Excerpts from Adoption Books for Adults.*

<u>FAVORITE CAUSES</u>

For Overseas Search & Reunion:
www.againstchildtrafficking.org

For Fundraising & Awareness:
www.againstchildtraffickingusa.org

<u>For Discussion:</u>

Find the "<u>Only in Adoption</u>" Survey at <u>AdoptionHistory.org</u>.
What do You Believe?

WHAT READERS ARE SAYING

For *Adoption Stories: Excerpts from Books for Adults*
"**Excellently written and researched.** The author does not sugar-coat the stories to make every adoption the salvation of a child. To some children, their parents were tricked, manipulated, or taken to be adopted. In reality, they sell some. Most of these stories are international adoptions. As adults, these Americans find out they have no real nationality because citizenship wasn't required for adoption."

"**I have found this book to be extremely moving...** I am not adopted and by the time I got to page five, I was already so excited to read this book, to learn more about the way the process works and how these adoptees feel, and to read the stories amongst them. I like the way that Janine has written it and how you can feel her authenticity just bleeding through the page."

For *the Search for Mother Missing:*

"**A Beautiful and Enlightening Journey.**"

"**Touched my heart.** I love that the authors tell this story in present tense. Feels like we're on the journey as it unfolds. As a bi-racial adoptee who grew up in the '80s and '90s, I related so much to the author. The section about not quite feeling connected is all too real. Especially the language barrier. When a stranger assumes you speak a language because of how you look, the feeling is of longing and disappointment. But this story inspires. There is pain, but it will also touch your heart."

"...I learned more about Korea and international adoption from this book than I've ever learned in 36 years of life. **The information was really enlightening.**"

"**I find this book written with warmth and sincerity.** It touched me. That is all that matters to me."

"**Enlightening. Wow, this was an interesting read.** I knew nothing about adoption, let alone foreign adoption prior to reading this thought-provoking and eye-opening book. I read it thinking it might be interesting and found myself shocked and amazed by what I read. This is a page-turner. If you are interested in learning more about adoption or just the journey of some of your fellow men, I highly recommend this book. It is entertaining, educational, and enlightening."

"**Informative and Affirming.**"

"*Adoption What You Should Know* **is a mind-blowing read**, considering that I have never thought about the adoption industry in this light. The evidence presented here is also overwhelming. As hinted earlier, parents looking to give their children up, adopting parents, and adoptees will learn a lot from reading this piece. Readers who love exposés will enjoy reading this book too."

Online Book Club

"**Wow. Just wow.**"

"**Brilliant exposure of where adoption and child trafficking collide.**"

I'd make this required reading for prospective parents. As a licensed clinical counselor, it's so encouraging to see an adoptee-led team work so hard to raise awareness about adoption. It also saddens me we have to work so hard to raise awareness about adoption. It takes time, heart and energy, boundless emotional labor to shift the antique adopter-centered narrative of adoption toward something better. The team at adoptiontruth is doing just that, and I cheer for them every step of the way. Thank you for this incredible work. I refer to it often in my clinical practice as I seek to raise consciousness about adoption-related reform and advocacy, both clinically in the field of mental health as well as within the walls of the local church.

"The Most Important Book in this Century"
Khara Nine Author of *Cries from the Soul*

"This was a really well-written book on adoption! There was a ton of research done, as well as I loved the historic references given by the author on the subject of adoption."

"Need to read if adoption is in your future. This is a very real subject; it's important to see all perspectives. This book does a wonderful job of going into personal experiences. It's a well-researched informative book that shows you the good, bad and ugly."

This book provides **great information** and a perspective that not everyone would have. As a former family law attorney, I've worked with adoptees that were looking for information on their birth parents as well as birth parents that were looking for their child. Adoption can be a heartbreaking event for some, but many benefit from it as our family has. However, it is good to have all perspectives, and I so appreciate this book.

Powerful Collection. This is a powerful and important read for all. The adoptee voice is all too often silenced, and it can literally be life or death for some to be heard and seen.

RARE ADOPTION BOOKS FOR ADULTS CAN BE FOUND HERE:

ANGUS & ROBERTSON | APPLE | BARNES & NOBLE | BOL.DE | BOOKMATE | CHINA | GOOGLE | INDIGO | KOBO | MONDADORI | ODILO | SCRIBD | THALIA.DE | VIVLIO | WALMART | 24 SYMBOLS

UNITED STATES | AUSTRALIA | BRAZIL | CANADA | DENMARK | FRANCE | INDIA | ITALY | JAPAN | MEXICO | NETHERLANDS | SPAIN | UNITED KINGDOM

Information is Power

Thirty-five pages of additional notes and resources, recommended videos, a book list, journal and newspaper articles, links to website resources, list of UN Conventions and Declarations; FBI sites on today's adoption trafficking, cases, and fraud, additional citations and sources.

UNITED NATIONS' CONVENTIONS AND DECLARATIONS:

http://www.un.org/en/decolonization/declaration.shtml
http://www.unodc.org/unodc/en/human-trafficking/what-is-human-trafficking.html?ref=menuside
http://www.ohchr.org/EN/ProfessionalInterest/Pages/CRC.aspx
http://www.unodc.org/unodc/en/organized-crime/index.html#what_organized_crime
http://www.unodc.org/unodc/en/human-trafficking/what-is-human-trafficking.html?ref=menuside
http://www.un.org/womenwatch/daw/cedaw/
http://www.hrweb.org/legal/cat.html
https://www.unicef.org/publications/files/Implementation_Handbook_for_the_Convention_on_the_Rights_of_the_Child_Part_1_of_3.p
http://www.un.org/esa/socdev/unpfii/documents/DRIPS_en.pdf

VIDEOS

NORTH AMERICA
An Adoptee's Nightmare: Domestic Adoptee from the US and *Adoptionland* contributor
https://www.youtube.com/watch?v=P7bTbFohMog

Baby Sellers. August 17, 2013. Director: Nick Willing. Inspired by true events, the Lifetime Original Movie, Baby Sellers, exposes the shocking international criminal enterprise of infant trafficking. Stars Emmy winner Jennifer Finnigan and Emmy and Golden Globe winner Kirstie Alley.

Canada's Home Children
https://www.youtube.com/watch?v=I-aDoWnK2Ic

Canada: Catholic Nuns forced women to give up babies for adoption or told moms newborn was 'dead'
https://www.youtube.com/watch?v=GnteXXMwedI

Does the State Ever Have a "Right" to Remove Children from a Home?
http://medicalkidnap.com/2015/01/26/does-the-state-ever-have-a-right-to-remove-children-from-a-home/
http://otoweb.cloudapp.net/timeline/mobile.htm

Fly Away Children Adopted from Ethiopia
https://www.youtube.com/watch?v=BP8tD2T6QEY

The Orphan Trains. Produced and Directed by: Graham, Janet and Gray, Edward. Perf: Charles Loring Brace IV, Matt Carlson, Dan Desmond, Moira Driscoll, Anthony Fusco, Susan Gordon-Clark, Rachel Miner, Amber Scott. Web. 2013.
http://www.pbs.org/wgbh/amex/orphan/orphans.html

Stolen Babies (1993) Georgia Tann's adoption scheme

https://www.youtube.com/watch?v=3NGFReg618s

http://raremovies.biz/inc/sdetail/12839

Stolen Child Presented by Hybrid. Inspired by True Story

https://www.youtube.com/watch?v=jktN8mA8y9M

Stolen Children | Residential School Survivors Speak **Out**
Native American adults speak about their childhoods away from family.

https://www.youtube.com/watch?v=vdR9HcmiXLA

EUROPE

Against Child Trafficking and Arun Dohle

https://www.youtube.com/channel/UC-jnRUCs6THHM4gkOGC_ebQ/videos?sort=dd&view=0&shelf_id=0 https://www.youtube.com/user/arundohle/videos

Forgotten Australians and British Children Abused by Nuns
On Australia, Britain and Commonwealth Nations:
https://www.youtube.com/watch?v=j9d5V64ftoU Search for "The Child Migration Scheme."

Norway's Stolen Children?
https://www.youtube.com/watch?v=C-PzrwliUk4

Oranges and Sunshine Oct. 8, 2010. Oranges and Sunshine tells the story of Margaret Humphreys, a social worker from Nottingham who uncovered one of the most significant social scandals of recent times: the deportation of thousands of children from the United Kingdom to Australia.

Philomena based on the 2009 investigative book by BBC correspondent Martin Sixsmith, and directed by Stephen Frears. Decades after an Irish-Catholic mother was forced into signing a contract that would not allow her any contact with her son, searches for her son sent away for adoption to the United States by church doctrine. Screenwriters: Steve Coogan and Jeff Pope.

Search a Child, Pay Cash: The Adoption Lobby
https://www.youtube.com/watch?v=y_Ebvs0HsEg

Slave Labour: Magdalene Laundries Disgraced Irish Catholic Women https://www.youtube.com/watch?v=hD9uffgeg7w

This World - Spain's Stolen Babies
https://www.youtube.com/watch?v=eJJ7Pp_Zvvs

ASIA

Cambodian Adoption Scandal

https://www.youtube.com/watch?v=Gfnja90whuI

(the Cambodian Adoption Scandal, involving Laury Galindo- the facilitator which Angelina Jolie used)

China's Stolen Children As many as 70,000 children snatched off the streets and sold by organized crime.
https://www.youtube.com/watch?v=o4WOIRL0RZo

Living with Dead Hearts Children reported missing in China
https://www.youtube.com/watch?v=Euttsy6QMm4 search

"Recovering What Was Left behind"
https://www.youtube.com/watch?v=p-a3d581hWA (Three contributors from *The "Unknown" Culture Club: Korean Adoptees Then and Now.*) http://www.dailymotion.com/video/x3dkj4x

Stolen and Sold Foreign Correspondent ABC Adopted from India https://www.youtube.com/watch?v=j5vFA-dUImw &
https://www.youtube.com/watch?v=YRON87JCcbU

Stolen Children, Stolen Lives, Part 1 on Palestinian Children
https://www.youtube.com/watch?v=9zaeERjVReE

The Mystery of the Missing Yemenite Children: A short report
https://www.youtube.com/watch?v=ewJfMk1bDRo

The Traffickers http://fusion.net/page/the-traffickers/

REFERENCES

Bean, Philip, and Melville, Joy. Lost Children of the Empire: The Untold Story of Britain's Child Migrants. London: Unwin Hyman Limited, 1989.

Berthrong, E.N. Ph.D. *What Would Confucius Do? Wisdom and Advice on Achieving Success and Getting Along with Others.* New York: Marlowe & Company, An Imprint of Avalon Publishing Group, 2005.

Bockian, Neil R.; Jongsma, Arthur E., Jr. *The Personality Disorders: Treatment Planner.* New York: John Wiley & Sons, Inc., 2001. Harmony Books, 2002.

Bowker, John. World Religions: The Great Faiths Explored and Explained. New York: DK Publishing, Inc., 1997.

Bradshaw, John. *Bradshaw on: The Family: A Revolutionary Way of Self Discovery.* Deerfield Beach, FL.: Health Communications Inc.,1988.

Bradshaw, John. *Reclaiming Virtue.* New York: Bantam Books, 2009.

Carangelo, Lori. Chosen Children 2016: People as Commodities in American's Failed Multi-Billion Dollar Foster Care, Adoption and Prison Industries. Access Press, 2016.

Coffey, Marilyn June. *Mail-Order Kid: An Orphan Train Rider's Story,* Nebraska: "out West" Press, 2001.

Colapinto, John. *As Nature Made Him: The Boy Who Was Raised as a Girl.* New York: HarperCollins/Publishers 2000.

DelBalzo, Jessica. Unlearning Adoption: A Guide to Family Preservation and Protection. Charleston, SC: Book Surge, 2007.

Dodds, Peter. *Outer Search Inner Journey: An Orphan and Adoptee's Quest.* Puyallup, WA: Aphrodite Publishing Company, 1997.

Dreher, Diane. *The Tao of Inner Peace*. New York: First HarperPerennial, 1990.

Dusky, Lorraine. *Birthmark*. New York. M.Evans & Co., 1979.

Dusky, Lorraine. *Hole in my Heart*. New York. Leto Media. 2015.

Dusky, Lorraine. *Still Unequal: The Shameful Truth About Women and Justice in America*. New York: Crown Publishers Inc., 1996.

Forward, Susan. *Toxic Parents: Overcoming Their Hurtful Legacy and Reclaiming Your Life*. New York: Bantam Books, 1989.

Fasulo, Linda. *An Insider's Guide to the UN*. New Haven and London: Yale University Press, 2003.

Fessler, Ann H. *The Girls Who Went Away: The Hidden History of Women Who Surrendered Children for Adoption in the Decades Before Roe v. Wade*. New York: Penguin Books, 2006.

Frankl, Viktor, E. *Man's Search for Meaning*, Revised and Updated. New York: Pocket Books a division of Simon & Schuster, 1959, 1962, 1984.

Gibbs, Nancy & Duffy, Michael. The Preacher and the Presidents: Billy Graham in the White House. New York: Center Street, 2007.

Goffman, Erving. *Stigma: Notes on the Management of Spoiled Identity*. New York: Simon & Schuster Inc. 1963

Harrop, Elizabeth Willmott. "Policy Makers' Attention Needed to Counter Intercountry Adoption." Think Africa Press. 2012. Online. http://www.againstchildtrafficking.org/2012/07/policy-makers%e2%80%99-attention-needed-to-counter-inter-country-adoption/#more-3067

Holt, Bertha. *Bring My Sons From Afar: The Unfolding of Harry Holt's Dream*. Eugene: Holt International Children's Services, 1986.

Holt, Mrs. Harry, as told to David Wisner. *The Seed from the East*. Los Angeles: Oxford Press, 1956.

To My Beloved Baby: Writings of Birth Mothers. Seoul, S. Korea: Holt Children's Services, Inc. 2005

Holt Children's Services, Inc. *We Believe in Miracles*. Seoul: Holt Children's Services, Inc., 2005.

Holt International Children's Services Press Release Tuesday, September 16th, 2003.

Hornby, Elfi. So, *This is America!* Federal Way, WA: Elfi Hornby, 2006.

Humphreys, Margaret. Empty Cradles: One Woman's Fight to Uncover Britain's Most Shameful Secret. London: Transworld Publishers LTD, 1994.

Joyce, Kathryn. The Child Catchers: Rescue, Trafficking and the New Gospel of Adoption. New York. PublicAffairs 2013

Ikeda, Daisaku. Learning from the Gosho: The Eternal Teachings of Nichiren Daishonin. World Tribune Press, 1997.

By the Editorial Staff of LIFE. *The World's Great Religion*. New York: Time, Inc., 1958.

Kim, Dr. David Hyunbok. *Who Will Answer...* Eugene, Ore: Holt International, 2006.

Korean American Historical Society. Han in the Upper Left: A Brief History of Korean Americans in the Pacific Northwest. Seattle: Chin Music Press, 2015.

Lauck, Jennifer. *Blackbird: A Childhood Lost and Found.* New York: Pocket Books, 2000.

Lee, Joong Keum Ph.D., Editor in Chief. *Korean War 1950.6.25 – 1953.7.27* Seoul: Woojung Books, 1015.

Maaga, Mary McCormick. Hearing the Voices of Jonestown: Putting a Human Face on an American Tragedy. Syracuse, New York: Syracuse University Press,1998.

McEnor, Rohan. *Rebecca's Law: Sojourn of a Stolen Father.* Gosford, Australia: Fuzzcapp Publishing, 1999.

McGreal, Ian P., Editor. *Great Thinkers of the Eastern World.* New York: Harper Collins Publisher, 1995.

Miller, Alice. *Thou Shalt Not Be Aware: Society's Betrayal of the Child.* New York: Farrar, Straus and Giroux, 1981.

Morrow, Dorothy. *The Gift of Roots.* http://thegiftofroots.com/overview.html (Paraphrase first portion)

Musser, Sandra Kay. I Would Have Searched Forever: A Birthmother's Search For The Child She Surrendered. Cape Coral: Adoption Awareness Press, 1979.

Myung Ja, Janine, and Moon Ja, Jenette. *The "Unknown" Culture Club: Korean Adoptees, Then and Now.* Seattle: Against Child Trafficking USA, 2015.

Myung Ja, Janine, Vance, Allen L. and Potter, Michael Allen. *Adoptionland: From Orphans to Activists,* Seattle: Against Child Trafficking USA, 2014.

Notovitch, Nicolas. *The Unknown Life of Christ: Infinite Knowledge of The Buddha.* Stepney, South Australia: Axiom Publishing, 2007.

O' Conner, Stephen. Orphan Trains: The Story of Charles Loring Brace and the Children He Saved and Failed. New York: Houghton Mifflin Books, 2001.

Palmer, John D. The Dance of Identities: Korean Adoptees and their Journey Toward Empowerment. Honolulu: University of Hawai'i Press, 2011.

Pilkington, Doris. Rabbit Proof Fence: The True Story of One of the Greatest Escapes of All Time. Australia: Queensland Press, 1996.

Post, Roelie. For Export Only: The 'Untold' Story of the Romanian Orphans. Netherlands: Hoekstra, St. Annaparochie, 2007.

Potter, Michael Allen. The Last Invisible Continent: Essays on Adoption and Identity. New York. Kartografisk Utgaver; 2nd edition. 2014.

Raymond, Barbara Bisantz. The Baby Thief: The Untold Story of Georgia Tann, the Baby Seller Who Corrupted Adoption. New York: Sterling Publishing Company, 2007.

Reiterman, Tim with Jacobs, John. Raven: The Untold Story of Rev. Jim Jones and His People. New York: Penguin Group, 1982.

Riben, Mirah. The Stork Market: America's Multi-Billion Dollar Unregulated Adoption Industry. Dayton, NJ: Advocate Publications, 2007.

Robinson, Evelyn. Adoption Separation, Then and Now. South Australia: Clova Publications, 2010.

Scheeres, Julia. A Thousand Lives: The Untold Story of Hope, Deception, and Survival at Jonestown. New York: Free Press, 2011.

Schein, Elyse and Bernstein, Paula. *Identical Strangers: A Memoir of Twins Separated and Reunited.* New York: Random House, 2007.

Sheler, Jeffrey L. Believers: A Journey into Evangelical America. New York. Penguin Group. 2006.

Stoen, Timothy Oliver. *Marked for Death: My War with Jim Jones the Devil of Jonestown.* North Charleston, South Carolina. Createspace 2015.

Tim Stoen's Testimony: Tim Stoen speaker for Men's Breakfast. Youtube. Uploaded by Rense Miller February 20, 2016.

Jonestown Massacre ' Stephan Jones. Stephan Jones, the 19-year-old son at the time of Reverend Jim Jones, talks about religion, drug addiction, and even wanting to murder his father. Uploaded by "Strombo." Uploaded 11, 2008.

Tzu, Lao (Introduction and Notes by Ong, Yi-Ping). *Tao Te Ching.* New York, NY: Barnes & Noble Classics, 2005.

Translated by Thurman, Robert A.F.. *The Tibetan Book of the Dead.* New York: Quality Paperback Book Club, a division of Bantam Doubleday Dell Publishing Group, 1994

Tolle, Eckhart. *The Power of Now: A Guide to Spiritual Enlightenment.* Novato California: New World Library, 1999.

Tolle, Eckhart. *The New Earth: Awakening to Your Life's Purpose.* New York. Penguin: Reprint edition. 2008.

Vance, Janine. The Search For Mother Missing: A Peek Inside International Adoption. Seattle: Missing Families Inc., 2007.

Wiesel, Elie. *Night.* New York: Hill and Wang, 1972, 1985.

Zhao, Xiaolan C.M.D. Ancient Healing for Modern Women: Traditional Chinese Medicine for All Phases of a Woman's Life. New York: Walker & Company

RESEARCH

Against Child Trafficking, "Fruits of Ethiopia." Intercountry Adoption: The Rights of the Child, or the "Harvesting" of Children?, commissioned by Wereldkinderen. October 2009

Americans for Open Records www.amfor.net "We believe all American citizens have the "right to know" what's in our records and to access and obtain what's ours and to correct any misinformation. AmFOR supports public access to such records and believes that denying public access threatens not only our personal security but also National Security and our Democracy."

Anderson, Rick. "His Past Life: An Old Molestation Allegation is Renewed Against the Former Head of Seattle's Children's Home." Seattle Weekly, 31 March 2004. Web. 4 Mar. 2008. <http://www.seattleweekly.com/news/0413/040331_news_mcg raw.php>

Asingh. "Asia's Orphanage Industry Worth Millions." Asian Pacific Post, 07 July 2015. Web. 15 Sept. 2015. <http://www.asianpacificpost.com/article/7013-asia%E2%80%99s-orphanage-industry-worth-millions.html>Baker, Mark. "Babies for Sale: No Warranty." The Sydney Morning Herald. 16, Dec. 2003. Web: 16, Nov. 2006. http://www.smh.com.au/articles/2003/12/15/1071336884728.h tml

Bose, Soumittra S. "Dutch Woman Finds Biological Mom in Bhandara After 27 Years." The Times of India, 8 Sept. 2015. Web. 11 Sept. 2015. <http://timesofindia.indiatimes.com/city/nagpur/Dutch-woman-finds-biological-mom-in-Bhandara-after-27-years/articleshow/48862033.cms>.

Carriere, Jeannine. "Promising Practice for Maintaining Identities in First Nation Adoption." First Peoples Child and Family Review. Volume 3, Number 1, 2007. pp. 46-64

Custer, Charles. "Kidnapped and Sold: Inside the Dark World of Child Trafficking in China." The Atlantic, 25 July 2013. Web. 6 Oct. 2015.
<http://www.theatlantic.com/china/archive/2013/07/kidnappe d-and-sold-inside-the-dark-world-of-child-trafficking-in-china/278107/>

Dewan, Shaila K. "Bertha Holt, 96, a Leader in International Adoptions." The New York Times. August 2, 2000.
http://www.nytimes.com/2000/08/02/us/bertha-holt-96-a-leader-in-international-adoptions.html

Dohle, Arun. "Inside Story of an Adoption Scandal." Samford University Cumberland Law Review – Volume 39:1. 13, November 2008. Web
<http://poundpuplegacy.org/node/28943>

Edmunds, Michelle. "Adopted Canadians Face Many Hurdles." Canadian Democratic Movement. 15, Aug. 2005. Web. 8 Nov. 2005. <http://www.canadiandemocraticmovement.ca/who-are-my-real-parents-what-is-my-ethnicity/>

Graff, E. J. "The Orphan Trade: A Look at Families Affected by Corrupt International Adoptions." Slate. 8, May 2009. Web. 14, Apr. 2009.
<http://www.slate.com/articles/news_and_politics/foreigners/ 2009/05/the_orphan_trade.htmlHua, Vanessa. "Korean-born in U.S. Return to a Home They Never Knew; Many Locate Lost Families." Chronicle. 11, Sept. 2005. Web. 12, Sept. 2005.
http://www.sfgate.com/news/article/Korean-born-in-U-S-return-to-a-home-they-never-2609323.php

"Independent Panel of Family Law Experts of EU Member States: Summary of Opinion on the Matter of Adoptions."

European Commission, Brussels. 19 May, 2004.
http://www.againstchildtrafficking.org/must-read-documents/

Lacey, Marc and Urbina, Ian. New York Times, Free Republic.
12, Feb. 2010. Web. "Detained Americans' Adviser Suspected of
Human Trafficking." The New York Times.
<http://www.wopular.com/adviser-detained-americans-haiti-
investigated-baptists.>

Maben, Scott. "Holt Agency President Quits." The Register-
Guard, 28 April 2004. Web. 6 June 2005.
<http://www.thefreelibrary.com/Holt+agency+president+quits.
-a0116096570>

National Sorry Day Committee. "Welcome to the National Sorry
Day Committee." 24, May. 2015. Web. http://www.nsdc.org.au/

Post, Roelie. "The Perverse Effects of the Hague Adoption
Convention." Against Child Trafficking. 2008. Web: 2011.

Seattle Times Staff. "Woman Gets 16 Years for Raping Daughter
From China." Seattle Times. 12, Mar. 2010. Web. 15, Mar. 2010.
<http://www.seattletimes.com/nation-world/woman-gets-16-
years-for-raping-daughter-from-china/>

Special Broadcasting System Australia (SBS) Timeline: Stolen
Generations. 26, Feb 2015.
http://www.sbs.com.au/news/article/2012/05/25/timeline-
stolen-generations

Tyre, Peg. "We Gave Him Up to Save His Life." New York
Magazine. Web. 4, Jan. 2007.
http://nymag.com/nymetro/urban/family/features/975/index1.
html#comments

Warren, Andrea. "The Orphan Train." The Washington Post
Company. 1998. Web: 18, July. 2015.

http://www.washingtonpost.com/wp-srv/national/horizon/nov98/orphan.htm.

Gillenson, Lewis W. *Billy Graham and Seven Who Were Saved*. New York: Trident Press, 1967.

Wilkerson, David. The Vision: A Terrifying Prophecy of Doomsday That is Starting to Happen Now. New York: Pyramid Books, 1974.

Ridenour, Fritz. *How to be a Christian in an UnChristian World*. Glendale, CA: G/L Publications, 1971.

Schonfield, Hugh J. Dr. *The Passover Plot: New Light on the History of Jesus*. New York: Bantam Book, 1965.

Scroggie, W. Graham. *Is the Bible the Word of God*. Chicago: Moody Press, 1922.

Lasor, William Sanford. *Men Who Knew Christ: Great Personalities of the New Testament*. Glendale, CA: G/L Publications, 1971.

Editor: Ridenour, Fritz. *Who Says God Created...* Glendale, CA: G/L Publications, 1971.

Lindsey, Hal. *There's a New World Coming*. New York: Bantam Books, 1973.

Anderson, Rick. "A Broke Home: A Legacy Children's Charity is in the Red, and it's not Clear How it Spent $2.3 million." Seattle Weekly News, Oct 9, 2006. http://archive.seattleweekly.com/2003-09-24/news/a-broke-home/

AcPf. *Africa: The New Frontier for Intercountry Adoption*. Addis Ababa: The African Child Policy Forum, 2012.

Askren, H.A., and K.C..Bloom "Post-Adoptive Reactions of the Relinquishing Mother: A Review." *Journal of Obstetric, Gynecological and Neonatal Nursing* 28, no. 4 (1999)

Dambach, Mia, and Christina Baglietto. Haiti: 'Expediting' Intercountry *Adoptions in the Aftermath of a Natural Disaster, Preventing Future Harm.* Geneva: International Social Service, 2010.

Documentary: *Fly Away Children.* Film Directed by Andrew Geoghegan. Sydney: Australian Broadcasting Corporation, 2009.

Fruits of Ethiopia: Intercountry Adoption: The Rights of the Child or the 'Harvesting' of Children. Brussels, Belgium: Against Child Trafficking. 2011.

"The Baby Business." Democracy Journal.

http://www.democracyjournal.org/17/67657.php?page=all

"Graff, E. J. "Anatomy of an Adoption Crisis." Foreign Policy, September 12, 2010.

Hubinette, Tobias. Comforting an Orphaned Nation: Representations of International Adoption and Adopted Koreans in Korean Popular Culture. Seoul: Jimoondang, 2006.

Selman, Peter. 'Global Trends in Intercountry Adoption: 2004 – 2010.' Newcastle University, England UK 2016.

Selman, Peter. 'Trends in Intercountry Adoption: Analysis of Data from 20 Receiving Countries, 1998–2004', Journal of Population Research, vol. 23, no. 2 (2006)

Siegal Rotabi, Karen. "From Guatemala to Ethiopia: Shifts in Intercountry Adoption Leaves Ethiopia Vulnerable for Child Sales and Other Unethical Practices." SW & S News Magazine (2010).

Siegal, Erin, Finding Fernanda: Two Mothers, One Child, and a Cross-Border Search for Truth. Oakland, CA: Cathexis Press, 2011.

Solinger, Rickie. Wake Up Little Susie: Single Pregnancy and Race before Roe v. Wade. New York: Routledge, 1992.

Wilson-Buterbaugh, Karen. "Research | Baby Scoop Era Research Initiative." Baby Scoop Era Research Initiative.

Balcom, Karen. The Traffic in Babies: Cross Border Adoption and Baby-Selling between The United States and Canada, 1930 - 1972. Toronto, ON: University of Toronto Press, 2011.

Lyslo, Arnold. "A Few Impressions on Meeting the Harry Holt Plane, the "Flying Tiger," Which Arrived in Portland, Oregon, December 27, 1958," pp. 1-2, 4-5, International Social Service, American Branch Papers, Box 10, Folder: "Children— Independent Adoption Schemes, Holt, Harry, vol. II 1958-1959," Social Welfare History Archives, University of Minnesota.

http://armyofone.me/tag/arnold-lyslo/
http://pages.uoregon.edu/adoption/archive/LysloHHP.html

http://www.seattlepi.com/local/article/Accused-ex-priest-led-Seattle-youth-home-1138810.php

http://mobile.nytimes.com/2015/01/18/magazine/why-a-generation-of-adoptees-is-returning-to-south-korea.html?smid=fb-nytimes

https://adoption.com/adoption-related-suicide-statistics-prevention

ENDNOTES:

[1]United Nations Human Rights Office of the High Commissioner
http://www.ohchr.org/EN/Issues/Pages/WhatareHumanRights.aspx
[2]Paullin, Charles O, Edited by John K. Wright (1932). Atlas of the
Historical Geography of the United States. New York, New York and
Washington, D.C.:: Carnegie Institution of Washington and
American Geographical Society. pp. Plate 42.
*Swindler, William F., Editor (1973–1979). Sources and Documents
of United States Constitutions.' 10 Volumes. Dobbs Ferry, New York:
Oceana Publications. pp. Vol. 10: 17–23.
*Van Zandt, Franklin K. (1976). Boundaries of the United States and
the Several States; Geological Survey Professional Paper 909.
Washington, D.C.: Government Printing Office. p. 92.
*How Virginia Got Its Boundaries, by Karl R Phillips
*Andrews, Charles M. (1924). *The Colonial Background of the
American Revolution.* New Haven and London: Yale University Press.
pp. 32–34.
[3]Hatch, Charles (1956). America's Oldest Legislative Assembly & Its
Jamestown Statehouses, Appendix II. Washington, D.C.: U.S.
Department of the Interior, National Park Service.
 *Bosher, Kate (1907). "The First House of Burgesses". The North
American Review. 184 (612): 733–39.
[4]Bean, Philip, and Meville, Joy. *Lost Children of the Empire: The
Untold Story of Britain's Child Migrants.* London: Unwin Hyman
Limited, 1989. Print. 37.
[5]Ibid., pg. 38-39
[6]Ibid., pg. 4
[7]Ibid., pgs. 4 -8, 11, 16, 18, 38-39
[8]Humphreys, Margaret. *Empty Cradles: One Woman's Fight to
Uncover Britain's Most Shameful Secret.* London: Transworld
Publishers LTD, 1994. Print. pg. 43
[9]Humphreys, pg. 57
[10]Ibid., Introduction
[11]Ibid., pgs. 41, 44, 56

[12]Indigenous Foundations Arts UBC Canada. The University of British Columbia. Copyright 2009. First Nations and Indigenous Studies. http://indigenousfoundations.arts.ubc.ca/home/government-policy/sixties-scoop.html

[13]Philp, Margaret (2002). "The Land of Lost Children," *The Globe and Mail*, Saturday, December 21, 2002, & Crey, Ernie, & Fournier, Suzanne (1998). *Stolen From Our Embrace. The Abduction of First Nations Children and the Restoration of Aboriginal Communities.* D&M Publishers Inc.

[14]http://www.childmigrantstrust.com/

[15]*Suche Kind, Zahle Bar – Die Adoptions lobby* by Golineh Atai, a German journalist, 2009. http://www.roeliepost.com/category/tv/

[16]Schuler, Thomas. "Child Wanted, Cash Paid." *The Atlantic Times*, 2010. https://www.scribd.com/document/28196274/Child-Wanted-Cash-Paid-Atlantic-Times-March-2010

[17]http://www.roeliepost.com/2010/03/child-wanted-cash-paid-the-shady-world-of-adoption-by-thomas-schuler/

[18]Schuler, Thomas. "Child Wanted, Cash Paid.' The Shady World of Adoption." *The Atlantic Times* March 2010. Theodora Bertzi, said in 2006 that this number was "not exaggerated."

[19]This article, "Adoption Under Fire," was first published in Dutch in November of 2008, in *Justitiële verkenningen*

[20]Post, Roelie. Romania: For Export Only. St. Anna Parochie, Netherlands: Hoekstra, 2007. Print. www.roeliepost.com 8, 2015 Posted September. "The EU's u-turn on children's rights: a pro-adoption biased interpretation of key international instruments." Against Child Trafficking. N.p., 08 Sept. 2015. "Article 21 of the United Nations Convention on the Rights of the Child: Adoption." Article 21 of the United Nations Convention on the Rights of the Child: Adoption | Pound Pup Legacy. N.p., n.d. Web.

[21]The U.S. Department of State Archive. Office of the Spokesman. Washington, DC. December 12, 2007. "United States Ratifies the Hague Convention on Intercountry Adoption." https://2001-2009.state.gov/r/pa/prs/ps/2007/dec/97148.htm

[22]Against Child Trafficking. "JCICS, US Adoption Trade Organisation Closure Confirmed!" Outgoing message from the JCICS. Wednesday, 24 June 2015. Board Chair, Brian Franklin. http://www.againstchildtrafficking.org/2015/06/jcics-us-adoption-trade-organisation-closure-confirmed/
[23]http://nobodyisforgotten.blogspot.com/2008/06/small-measure-of-justice-for-masha.html
https://www.childlaw.us/child_exploitation_cracks_in/#.X1U0U-eSmUk
https://www.dailybastardette.com/jcics-racist-ad-draw-ire-of-adoptees-and-adoptive-parents/
http://www.dailybastardette.com/jcics-attempts-to-flood-net-and-russia-with-positive-adoption-stories/
David M. Smolin. "Child Laundering As Exploitation: Applying Anti-Trafficking Norms to Intercountry Adoption Under the Coming Hague Regime" *ExpressO* (2007) Available at: http://works.bepress.com/david_smolin/4/
ABC News, Heroic Young Girl Tells of Her Child Porn Ordeal, Dec. 1, 2005, available at: http://abcnews.go.com/Primetime/LegalCenter/story?id'1364110
David Conti, Child Abuse 'monster' gets 35-70 years, Pittsburgh Tribune Review, November 18, 2005, available at http://www.pittsburghlive.com/x/pittsburghtrib/s_395759.html
http://poundpuplegacy.org/node/7490
http://poundpuplegacy.org/files/FocusOnAdoptionMission.pdf
[24]Reverend Jim Jones, cult leader and adoptive father best known for spearheading the Jonestown Massacres (also known for shaming and guilting his congregation into adopting), depended upon his followers to "stay positive" in their new home in Guyana, South America. This zealous attitude of avoidance regarding blatant abuse eventually led "his people" to their deaths. In a forthcoming book, I incorporate FBI transcripts of the reverend and his wife at the time of receiving two Korean-born children during a televised church event. Later on, both children died: one in a car accident soon after obtainment; and the other during the Jonestown massacre. I also include a telephone transcript of the third Korean-born adoptee's

conversation with Reverend Jim Jones' wife (the children's adoptive mother) reflecting the young woman's opinion on her adoption placement with this infamous couple who flaunted images of themselves as a "rainbow family."

[25]Brace, Charles Loring. "The Life of Charles Loring Brace: Chiefly told in his own Letters." New York: C. Scribners Sons. 1894. http://iiif.lib.harvard.edu/manifests/view/drs:4898539$44i

[26]Brace, Charles Loring. The life of Charles Loring Brace :chiefly told in his own letters. New York : C. Scribner's Sons, 1894. CHAPTER VI page 157 - 158 (seq. 172) Collection Development Department, Widener Library, HCL Harvard University 09 April 2016 http://nrs.harvard.edu/urn-3:FHCL:920265?n=172

[27]Brace, Charles Loring. The life of Charles Loring Brace :chiefly told in his own letters. New York : C. Scribner's Sons, 1894. CHAPTER VI page 157 - 158 (seq. 172) Collection Development Department, Widener Library, HCL Harvard University 09 April 2016 http://nrs.harvard.edu/urn-3:FHCL:920265?n=172

[28]"American Experience." American Experience . The Orphan Trains Transcript | PBS. N.p., n.d.. http://www.pbs.org/wgbh/amex/orphan/orphants.html

[29]Harvard pg. 159

[30]Stephen O'Conner *Orphan Trains: The Story of Charles Loring Brace and the Children He Saved and Failed*. Houghton Mifflin Company. *New York. 2001* Introduction

[31]http://www.kancoll.org/articles/orphans/or_homes.htm (97 charities placed out) "Orphan train riders, offspring seek answers about heritage" USA Today http://usatoday30.usatoday.com/news/parenting-family/adoption/story/2012-01-24/Orphan-train-riders-offspring-seek-answers-about-heritage/52779412/1

[32]Coffey, Marilyn June. *Mail-Order Kid: An Orphan Train Rider's Story*, Nebraska: "out West" Press, 2001. Introduction: xix

[33]Dianne Creagh, "The Baby Trains: Catholic Foster Care and Western Migration, 1873-1929," Journal of Social History (2012) 46#1 pp 197-218

"Orphan Trains The Story of Charles Loring Brace and the Children He Saved and Failed." The New York Times. The New York Times, n.d. Web. 27 Apr. 2017.
<http://www.nytimes.com/books/first/o/oconnor-01orphan.html>.
[34]Ibid., pgs. 17 - 20
[35]Ibid., pg. 17
[36]Coffey, Marilyn June. *Mail-Order Kid: An Orphan Train Rider's Story*, Nebraska: "out West" Press, 2001. Print. pg. 34
[37]Ibid., pgs. 197 -199
[38]Brennan, Emily. "New York Adoptees Fight for Access to Birth Certificates." *The New York Times.* June 15, 2014.
http://www.nytimes.com/2014/06/16/nyregion/adopted-children-fight-for-access-to-birth-certificates.html?_r=0
http://bastards.org/bb-know-thine-enemies/
[39]http://www.commercialappeal.com/entertainment/author-spent-16-years-delving-into-the-power-georgia-tann-wielded-and-the-victims-she-left-ep-398841-323991321.html
[40]Raymond, Barbara Bisantz. *The Baby Thief: The Untold Story of Georgia Tann, the Baby Seller Who Corrupted Adoption.* New York: Sterling Publishing Company, 2007. Print. pg. 46
[41]Ibid., pgs. 47 - 48
[42]"Welcome House: A Historical Perspective". Pearl S. Buck International. *Retrieved 2015-04-06.*
[43]Raymond pg. 101
[44]Ibid., pgs. 109 -110, 115
[45]According to the Economic and Social Affairs from the United Nations report on Child Adoptions: Trends and Policies (2009), all nations except for twelve, allow for single men to adopt. Adult intercountry adoptees who are aware of this, find it shocking that overseas adoptions are considered better protection for children or deemed *in the child's best interest* over the idea for these children staying in their own homes and their own communities.
[46]Raymond pg. 101
[47]Ibid., pg. 139
[48]Ibid., pg. 118
[49]Ibid., pgs. 102 – 108. 118, 139

[50]Browning, Maria. "She Terrified People: Finally, a book tells the story of Tennessee's infamous baby seller." July 17, 2008. Nashville Scene. http://www.nashvillescene.com/nashville/she-terrified-people/Content?oid=1197170
Note on *The Baby Thief:* On adoptee forums, a few US-born domestic adoptees voiced being bothered that the book was written by an adoptive parent who vied for closed adoption records and was "as vengeful as Tann was." They were bothered that adopters are, "hogging all the attention." *The Baby Thief* was made into a television movie, called *Stolen Babies*, starring Mary Tyler Moore.
[51]D'Arcy, Claudia Corrigan. "Interviewing with Dan Rather Reports." Musings of the Lame, April 8, 2012. http://www.adoptionbirthmothers.com/interviewing-with-dan-rather-reports/
[52]Joyce, Katherine. *The Child Catchers: Rescue, Trafficking and the New Gospel of Adoption.* PublicAffairs[TM]. New York. 2013. pg. 100
[53]"More than six million American mothers surrendered children for adoption. In the wake of Oregon's decision to open records, society has a renewed interest in these heretofore invisible women. America has been unwilling to look behind the scenes at adoption practices. After all, adoption is so sacred that it was enshrined on a postage stamp. Myths surround these mothers, who are either cast as sacrificial heroines or vilified as unnatural women who abandoned babies. Society believes that these mothers willingly gave up their babies and that they want privacy from their adult children. Fact is, these women long for contact and were never promised privacy.
It is important to hear this story so you understand that these women were pressured on all sides into surrendering their children and that in many cases their human rights were violated. I know this story because it is my story and the story of many others like me."
"When a mother loses her child to closed adoption, it feels as if her child has died, yet there is no wake, no funeral, no sympathy cards, no public acknowledgement. There are no friends or relatives to offer comfort and support. There is no obituary, no grave to visit, no

flowers to bring, no grieving permitted and no closure." "The Baby Scoop Era (BSE) "Adoption History – Setting the Record Straight" by Karen Wilson Buterbaugh first published in Moxie Magazine, April 6, 2001. http://www.originsamerica.org/adoption-articles/the-baby-scoop-era-bse/

[54]Professor Elizabeth J. Samuels from the Baltimore School of Law

[55]Raymond (104)

[56]Samuels, Elizabeth J., How Adoption in America Grew Secret; Birth Records Weren't Closed for the Reasons You Might Think (October 21, 2001). Washington Post, p. B.05, Sunday, October 21, 2001. Available at SSRN: http://ssrn.com/abstract=1282262

[57]Andrews, Valerie. "Language of Adoption" in the category of Adoption Practices. Origins, Canada. "Birthmothers" are a contemporary construction. In fact, "birthmothers" did not exist before the 1970s. The term "birthmother" was devised by adoption professionals to reduce a woman to a biological function. This term marginalizes mothers and creates a role for them in society which does not allow them to fully embrace their lived experience as a mother. The term also implies that the bond of mother and child within adoption, ends at birth. The earliest recorded use of the terms "birthmother" and "birth parents" are in articles written by adoptive parent Pearl S. Buck in 1955, 1956, and 1972. They were further used in articles published between 1974 and 1976 by adoption workers Annette Baran and Reuben Pannor and social work professor Arthur Sorosky (Origins Canada, 2011)." Andrews also includes two pertinent quotes: "Language is very powerful. Language does not just describe reality. Language creates the reality it describes." from Desmond Tutu and "Language can be discriminatory when we fail to consider the assumptions which inform the words we use. It expresses cultural norms and belief systems which are often so entrenched in language as to appear 'normal', or 'true'. "Watch your Language", University of Melbourne "Adoption Statistics". The Adoption History Project. University of Oregon. Retrieved 17 October 2014.

[58]*Once Removed: Voices from Inside the Adoption Triangle*, Redmond, Sleightholm 1982.

[59]*Adoption Wisdom*, by Marlou Russell, Ph.D.
[60]http://home.att.net/~judy.kelly/SResults...
http://unlockingtheheart.com/www/A_resources.htm
viii & ix : introduction. "many involving children she had kidnapped."
[61]"Because those of us in a crisis pregnancy are faced with stress, fear and loss, we're naturally prone to denial. That's one thing that makes thinking clearly about adoption so tricky. Another is that it's very hard to accurately imagine what adoption will be like. You really don't know until you've done it—and in many states, once you give your right to parent to someone else, there is no turning back. We at Concerned United Birthparents feel it's the duty of every birthparent to share what we wish we had known when we were considering adoption. The words that follow are not intended to be anti-adoption. The fact is that adoption might well be the best plan for you and your child—but in order to be a truly good thing, it needs to be a well-considered decision, made at least twice—once before the birth, once after. Your decision will not be fully informed unless you hear the negative aspects of adoption as well as the positive. Following are the most common regrets birthparents have voiced." 1) I wish I had known that family preservation should come first. 2) I wish I had known the extent to which adopted children deal with issues of abandonment. 3) I wish I had known that I wasn't carrying my child for someone else, and that it wasn't my responsibility to help the infertile couples of the world. 4) I wish I had known that society dislikes and fears birthparents. 5) "I wish I had known the ways in which agency adoptions may be safer than private adoptions. 6) I wish I had known that professionals who say they are there to help you are in actuality serving the real client, the prospective adoptive parent. 7) "I wish I had known that numerous internet resources exist for birthmothers and women in crisis pregnancies to find each other and talk. 8) "I wish I had known the difference between a truly open adoption and a semi-open one. 9. "I wishI had known that in most states, open adoption agreements are not legally enforceable. "I wish I had known there was no need to rush my decision; that it could have waited until after the birth." 11) "I wish I had known how much I was going to love my child." 12)

"I wish I had known that the pain of adoption never goes away." 13) "I wish I had known that the effects of adoption are so far-reaching. 14) "I wish I had known that in putting my baby first, I didn't have to put myself last." Ganz, Sheila. "Unlocking the Heart of Adoption: Bridging the gap between birth and adoptive families." San Francisco, CA. 2015. For a brochure on the aforementioned list, go to: http://hslowe.tripod.com/BOOKLET.pdf at http://unlockingtheheart.com/www/A_resources.htm

[62]Nemy, Enid. "Adopted Children Who Wonder, 'What Was Mother Like?' The New York Times, July 25, 1972. https://www.nytimes.com/1972/07/25/archives/adopted-children-who-wonder-what-was-mother-like.html

[63] Dusky, "Yearning," The New York Times, March 1, 1975.

[64] Dusky, "A Natural Mother Speaks Out on Adoptees' Right to Know," Town & Country, October 1976.

[65] Assembly: Sealed Adoption Records and Identity, April 28, 1976. Retrieved: http://web.archive.org/web/20081109045659/http:/www.bastards.org/activism/local/ny/hearings.html

[66] Wayne Carp, Family Matters, Secrecy and Disclosure in the History of Adoption (Cambridge, MA and London, 1998), p. 205.

[67] Carp, pps. 179-180.

[68] Carp, p. 185.

[69] Judy Klemesrud, "Mothers Find the Children They Gave Up," The New York Times, August 29, 1983, B 5.

[70]DeMeyer, Trace. *One Small Sacrifice: Lost Children of the Indian Adoption Projects.* Blue Hand Books, Greenfield, Massachusetts. 2010/2012. Second Edition. (Out of Print. Author now known as Trace Lara Hentz).

[71]pg. 64 -65

[72]Riben, Mirah. "The Insensitivity of Adoption Day Celebrations." Huffington Post. 5.06.15 http://www.huffingtonpost.com/mirah-riben/the-insensitivity-of-adoption-day-celebrations_b_7207100.html Hicks, Patrick. 'Gotcha Day,' Meeting Your Adopted Child.' Huffington Post.4.27.15.

http://www.huffingtonpost.com/patrick-hicks/gotcha-day-meeting-your-adopted-child_b_7102480.html

Riben, Mirah. "Adoptees and the Original Parents Speak Out About National Adoption Awareness Month (NAAM) Huffington Post. 10.29.16 http://www.huffingtonpost.com/entry/adoptees-and-the-original-parents-speak-out-about-national_us_58155e30e4b09b190529c5e8

[73]Jacobs, Margeret. A Generation Removed (Lincoln: University of Nebraska Press, 2014).

*Bureau of Indian Affairs Press Release, March 14, 1966.

Palmiste, Claire. "From the Indian Adoption Project to the Indian Child Welfare Act: the resistance of Native American communities," Indigenous Policy Journal Vol. XXII, No. 1 (Summer 2011) http://upstanderproject.org/firstlight/iap

*A minimum of 25 percent of all Indian children are either in foster homes, adoptive homes, and or boarding schools. Senator James Abourezk, 1977 Senate Hearing.

Joyce, Kathryn. "The Adoption Crunch, The Christian Right, and the Challenge to Indian Sovereignty." Political Research Associates. February 23, 2014. http://www.politicalresearch.org/2014/02/23/the-adoption-crunch-the-christian-right-and-the-challenge-to-indian-sovereignty/

[74]Gibbs, Nancy & Duffy, Michael. The Preacher and the Presidents: Billy Graham in the White House. New York: Center Street, 2007. pg. 22

[75]Ibid., pg. 15

[76]Ibid., pg. 16

[77]Ibid., pg. 11

[78]Gibbs, Nancy & Duffy, Michael. The Preacher and the Presidents: Billy Graham in the White House. New York: Center Street, 2007.

[79]Billy Graham Evangelical Association Billy Graham.org Media Resources and Press Kit. The website offers a list of archived television sermons. http://billyGraham.org/tv-and-radio/television/classics/

[80]Statement from my adoptive father, a former choir director, Sunday school teacher, youth group leader, Boy Scout leader, and ruling elder and fan of Billy Graham.

[81]"BGEA History." Billy Graham Evangelistic Association. N.p., n.d. Web. 28 Apr. 2017. <https://billygraham.org/news/media-resources/electronic-press-kit/bgea-history/>.

[82]Media website Resource page from Billy Graham's news. "Timeline of Historic Events." Gives a listing of significant crusades, rallies, broadcasts and expansion from 1947 to 2013.
http://billyGraham.org/news/media-resources/electronic-press-kit/bgea-history/timeline-of-historic-events/
*https://faithinspires.wordpress.com/2016/09/03/new-film-from-the-billy-graham-evangelistic-associations-my-hope-ministry-launched-online-sept-1/

[83]Gillenson, Lewis W. *Billy Graham and Seven Who Were Saved.* New York: Trident Press, 1967. Pg. 8

[84]"For one more revival, rise up Korean churches, remembering Billy Graham in Korea 1970s."
https://www.youtube.com/watch?v=qFJVdAQi8Ko Retrieved June 2016.

[85]Pollock, John. The Billy Graham Story: Revised and Updated Edition of To All the Nations by Rev. Dr. John Charles Pollock. Grand Rapids, MI: Zondervan, Nov. 16, 2003. Pg. 122. Print.

[86]"1973, Billy Graham," uploaded by cmimediaus. Retrieved June 2016. https://www.youtube.com/watch?v=uFCPTPx5380

[87]Pollock, John. The Billy Graham Story: Revised and Updated Edition of To All the Nations by Rev. Dr. John Charles Pollock. Grand Rapids, MI: Zondervan, Nov. 16, 2003. Pg. 122. Print.

[88]June 3, 1973: Billy Graham Preaches to 1.1 million in Korea - The Billy Graham Library Blog." The Billy Graham Library. N.p., 02 Mar. 2016. Web. 28 Apr. 2017. <https://billygrahamlibrary.org/june-3-1973-billy-graham-preaches-to-1-1-million-in-korea/>.
https://billygrahamlibrary.org/june-3-1973-billy-graham-preaches-to-1-1-million-in-korea/

[89]The Seattle Times. "Billy Graham To Visit Seattle And Tacoma." Saturday, October 13, 1990.

http://community.seattletimes.nwsource.com/archive/?date=1990
1013&slug=1097999
United Press International "Billy Graham Begins Weeklong
Crusade." May 15, 1983.
http://www.upi.com/Archives/1983/05/15/Billy-Graham-begins-
week-long-crusade/4352421819200/
[90]Graham, Ruth "So You Want to Adopt" The 700 Club c/o Christian
Broadcasting Network.
http://www.cbn.com/700club/guests/bios/ruth_Graham092206.as
px?mobile=false
[91]"Ruth Graham: When Your Daughter Says 'I'm Pregnant.'"
Christian Broadcasting Network. Retrieved 2016.
 http://www1.cbn.com/700club/ruth-Graham-when-your-daughter-
says-im-pregnant
[92]Yi Sun-ae, *Peurancheseuka Ri Seutori* (Seoul: Raendeom Hauseu
Jungang, 2005).
[93]In February 1933, Rhee met Austrian Franziska Donner in Geneva.
At the time, Rhee was participating in a League of Nations meeting
and Donner was working as an interpreter. In October 1934, they
were married in New York City. She also acted as his secretary. They
adopted a boy, Rhee In-soo Yi In-su or 이인수 - (b. September 1,
1931). In 1960, the 84-year-old Rhee won his fourth term in office
as President with 90% of the vote. His presidency ended in
resignation following popular protests against a disputed election.
On April 28, 1960, a DC-4 belonging to the United States Central
Intelligence Agency and operated by Civil Air Transport, covertly
flew Rhee out of South Korea. The former president, his Austrian-
born wife Franziska Donner, and adopted son then lived in exile in
Honolulu, Hawaii, U.S. On July 19, 1965, Rhee died of a stroke at the
age of 90.
프란체스카 [Francesca]. Encyclopedia of Korean culture (in
Korean). Academy of Korean studies. [李承晚] [Rhee Syngman].
Doopedia (in Korean). Doosan Corporation. Retrieved March 12,
2014.
https://www.everipedia.com/Syngman_Rhee/

[94]Bishop, Bill. The Register-Guard. June 1984.
https://news.google.com/newspapers?nid=1310&dat=19840619&i
d=X2sVAAAAIBAJ&sjid=keEDAAAAIBAJ&pg=5586,4781019&hl=en
http://poundpuplegacy.org/node/32600
[95]http://www.medicaldaily.com/adopted-teens-4-times-more-likely-
attempt-suicide-stark-reminder-clinicians-should-take-parental
http://pediatrics.aappublications.org/content/pediatrics/early/2013
/09/04/peds.2012-3251.full.pdf
http://www.tobiashubinette.se/
[96]This couple happened to be married first cousins. Baker, Mark.
"Children Changing Lives." The Register-Guard. 2006. Gale Group, a
Thomson Corporation Company.
https://www.thefreelibrary.com/Children+changing+lives.-
a0153322085
[97]Holt, Bertha. *Bring My Sons From Afar: The Unfolding of Harry
Holt's Dream.* Eugene: Holt International Children's Services, 1986.
Print. (13)
[98]World Vision, Inc. "Dead Men On Furlough 1954 with Bob Pierce."
Uploaded by World Vision Video Department. (2012)
https://vimeo.com/37189667
[99]Holt pg. 11 -12
[100]Holt pg. 16
[101]Holt pgs. 27, 81, 102
[102]Dodds, Peter F. (2015) "The Parallels between International
Adoption and Slavery," *Sociology Between the Gaps: Forgotten and
Neglected Topics*: Vol. 1 , Article
10. Available at:
http://digitalcommons.providence.edu/sbg/vol1/iss1/10
[103]Joyce, Kathryn. "Orphan Fever: The Evangelical Movement
Adoption Obsession: When devout Christian families made it their
mission to save children from war-torn countries, the match was
often far from heavenly." *Mother Jones.* May/June 2013
http://www.motherjones.com/politics/2013/04/christian-
evangelical-adoption-liberia
[104]Kim, Dr. David Hyungbok. *Who Will Answer...* Eugene. Holt
International. 2006 pg. 122

[105]Nehrbass, Daniel Ph. D., President of Nightlight Christian Adoptions. "Adoption PREVENTS Trafficking." https://www.nightlight.org/2016/02/adoption-prevents-trafficking/ & https://adoption.com/Prevent-trafficking-adopt

[106]Kim, Dr. David Hyungbok. *Who Will Answer...* Eugene. Holt International. 2006 pg. 254

[107]The New York Times. "Harry Holt, Who Found Parents For 3,000 Korean Orphans, Dies; Oregon farmer is Stricken at 59 Near Seoul on New Adoption' Trip." April 29, 1964. http://www.nytimes.com/1964/04/29/harry-holt-who-found-parents-for-3000-korean-orphans-dies.html?_r=0

[108]Kim pgs. 102, 106, 108, 122, 199, 200, 254, 217, 370, 371

[109]San Diego State University. Department of Religious Studies. "Alternative Considerations of Jonestown and Peoples Temple" at Jonestown Institute. Q415 Summary prepared by Fielding M. McGehee III.
http://jonestown.sdsu.edu/?page_id=27453 Audio of Reverend Jim and Marceline Jones' obtainment of Lew Eric and Stephanie Audio of Reverend Jim and Marceline Jones' obtainment of Lew Eric and Stephanie Jones I checked with Korean organizations regarding the comment that lepers from South Korea searched for and ate children so that the lepers could "grow back their limbs," an accusation made by the television host later on in the recording, which motivated westerners to apply for children. This is one of many lies made against the Koreans that added to the defamation of their character, justifying the evangelical child market for intercountry adoption. ADDITIONAL NOTE: In the 1950s, just after the Korean War, the natives were left with the impression that the orphanages served as child welfare stations (or hospital or sanctuary), which would provide temporary care until they could get back on their feet (or get their finances in order). This trust is the reason many of the children were "abandoned" there. Today, Korean adoptees are discovering that their families had gone back to request for their children, unprepared for the permanent separation. They found that the children had already been sent overseas for intercountry adoption without any notification

whatsoever. Staff members never considered inviting families inside the facilities (or to provide resources to keep families intact). The citizens were led to believe that the foreign charities could only care for children. Due to poverty and disempowerment, the parents did not have the audacity to ask if they, too, could receive assistance.
[110]Dan Rather's 2014 program on AXS TV, "Unwanted in America: The Shameful Side of International Adoption. Commentary can be found from Mirah Riben at Huffington Post: http://www.huffingtonpost.com/mirah-riben/preventing-unadoption-tragedies_b_6325132.html
[111]And pertinent comments on the forum. A favorite by an adoptee: "Acts of benevolence by the color-blind privileged add yet another layer of violence to the personhood of vulnerable little people, compounding their losses. The redistribution of children of color is rooted in the marginalization of ethnic groups and the propensity to make fetish objects of their children. It is no charity to exploit a time of tragedy – or any time – to take a nation's most valuable resource for personal gain. It is a sad statement when those that capitalize on tragedy pat themselves on the back for their charity. The truly charitable would offer to help victims to help themselves. This feeding frenzy we are witnessing today by would-be child importers truly reveals the darkest aspects of man's ability to rationalize the ugliest of acts. It's high time we respect the humanity of all peoples by preserving families and allowing them the dignity to build their own strong societies without the intervention of self-interested parties. THAT would be the action of an enlightened, advanced, civil society." https://forbiddenfamily.com/tag/keep-siblings-together-in-haiti/
[112]Pirani, Salima. "Adoption is not the Answer." International Adoption Facts. November 2, 2006.
First posted http://www.thestar.com/printArticle/114406. But also can be found, here: https://sites.google.com/site/internationaladoptionfacts/adoption-is-not-the-answer
[113]"American would-be adopters, the Catholic Church, international adoption agencies and independent adoption facilitators applied

pressure on the Haitian government in order to airlift the alleged orphans before anyone could confirm whether their parents or relatives are still alive -- At this writing, the first 500 or so alleged orphans were airlifted to the U.S. (according to the U.S. State Department)and 900 children were in process of being adopted from Haiti and placed in U.S. homes."
http://www.amfor.net/babybrokers/#haiti
[114]Excerpted from Afrikan World News: Assata Shakur Forums. http://www.assatashakur.org/forum/afrikan-world-news/41387-u-s-citizens-arrested-children-taken-haiti-without-permission.html and commentary from http://www.amfor.net/babybrokers/#haiti
[115]Lacey, Marc. "Haiti Charges Americans With Child Abduction." The New York Times. The New York Times, 04 Feb. 2010. Web. 27 Apr. 2017.
<http://www.nytimes.com/2010/02/05/world/americas/05orphans.html?pagewanted=all&_r=0>.
Bajak, Frank. "Orphan Rescue' attempt hits nerve among Haitians" Boston.com. The Boston Globe, 01 Feb. 2010. Web. 27 Apr. 2017.
<http://archive.boston.com/news/world/latinamerica/articles/2010/02/01/orphan_rescue_attempt_hits_nerve_among_haitians/>.
Excerpted from Afrikan World News: Assata Shakur Forums. http://www.assatashakur.org/forum/afrikan-world-news/41387-u-s-citizens-arrested-children-taken-haiti-without-permission.html and commentary from at http://www.amfor.net/babybrokers/#haiti
Sundby, Alex. "Haiti: Americans Improperly Took Children." CBS News. CBS Interactive, 30 Jan. 2010. Web. 27 Apr. 2017.
<http://www.cbsnews.com/news/haiti-americans-improperly-took-children/>.
"Haiti PM says US missionaries knew they were doing wrong." The Telegraph. Telegraph Media Group, 02 Feb. 2010. Web. 27 Apr. 2017.
<http://www.telegraph.co.uk/news/worldnews/centralamericaandthecaribbean/haiti/7132399/Haiti-PM-says-US-missionaries-knew-they-were-doing-wrong.html>.
Port-au-Prince, Nick Allen in. "Haiti earthquake: voodoo high priest claims aid monopolised by Christians." The Telegraph. Telegraph

Media Group, 01 Feb. 2010. Web. 27 Apr. 2017.
<http://www.telegraph.co.uk/news/worldnews/centralamericaandt
hecaribbean/haiti/7119572/Haiti-earthquake-voodoo-high-priest-
claims-aid-monopolised-by-Christians.html>.
[116]https://www.uscis.gov/tools/glossary/orphan, The definition of
orphan according to the U.S. Citizenship and Immigration Services.
The Immigration and Nationality Act provides a definition of an
orphan for the purposes of immigration to the United States: "A
child may be considered an orphan because of the death or
disappearance of, abandonment or desertion by, or separation or
loss from, both parents. The child of an unwed mother or surviving
parent may be considered an orphan if that parent is unable to care
for the child properly and has, in writing, irrevocably released the
child for emigration and adoption. The child of an unwed mother
may be considered an orphan, as long as the mother does not marry
(which would result in the child having a stepfather) and as long as
the child's biological father has not legitimated the child. If the
father legitimates the child or the mother marries, the mother is no
longer considered a sole parent. The child of a surviving parent may
also be an orphan if the surviving parent has not married since the
death of the other parent (which would result in the child's having a
stepfather or stepmother)."
[117]Stewart, Kerry. "Is Voluntourism the New Colonialism?" ABC
Network Australia. Monday, March 24, 2014.
http://www.abc.net.au/radionational/programs/encounter/534138
4
[118]Australian Government response to the Senate Committee
Inquiry Attorney-General's Department.
https://www.ag.gov.au/About/ForcedAdoptionsApology/Pages/Aus
tralianGovernmentresponsetotheSenateCommitteeInquiry.aspx
[119]"Adoption Lobby Alert: Counselling on how to give Informed
Consent for Intercountry Adoption."
The new "Hague Adoption Convention" way to relinquish children.
Instead of subsidiarity (adoption as a last resort), parents can
directly [and naively] free their children for intercountry adoption.
And no other help or options are offered."

http://www.againstchildtrafficking.org/2015/11/adoption-lobby-
alert-counselling-on-how-to-give-informed-consent-for-
intercountry-adoption/

[120]Akafate, Roman. *Winning Life in America: by Achieving One
Success at a Time. The Ethiopian Orphan Who Made It in America.*
Edited and formatted by Princeton Commercial Holdings.
Washington State. 2011.

[121]Akafate pg. 61, 79, 83 – 84, 88

[122]http://www.againstchildtrafficking.org/2014/03/jcics-conference-
call-adoptions-gone-
toxic/http://www.againstchildtrafficking.org/wp-
content/uploads/Conference-Call-JCICS-March-2014-Full-
Transcript.pdf

[123]Reader reviews on Goodreads.
http://www.goodreads.com/book/show/675331.To_Train_Up_a_C
hild

[124]US Department of State, Bureau of Consular Affairs on
Intercountry Adoption Statistics
https://travel.state.gov/content/adoptionsabroad/en/about-
us/statistics.html

[125]JCICS presented themselves as another advocacy group for
children, but because of Against Child Trafficking's proficiency, it has
become evident that it was simply another voice for the adoption
industry.

[126]Against Child Trafficking. "JCICS, US Adoption Trade Organisation
Closure Confirmed." Retrieved Online 7.15
http://www.againstchildtrafficking.org/2015/06/jcics-us-adoption-
trade-organisation-closure-confirmed/

[127]Hosseini, Bijan. "Ethiopia Bans Foreign Adoptions." CNN, Cable
News Network,
3 Feb. 2018. https://www.cnn.com/2018/01/11/africa/ethiopia-
foreign-adoption-ban/index.html?no-
st=1540382618&fbclid=IwAR1KborpOZxpSA6d5ZbygDpKBZfVlhMND
_XCnQOq0-Jv5yTuJYAyNlhM5AQ

[128]Australian Human Rights Commission. "Bringing Them Home: The
'Stolen Children' Report (1997)

http://www.humanrights.gov.au/our-work/aboriginal-and-torres-strait-islander-social-justice/publications/bringing-them-home-stolen
http://stolengenerationstestimonies.com/index.php
Marten, J.A.. Children and War, NYU Press, NY p.229.
Indigenous Australians make up about 2.6% of Australia's population.
[129]My research into the practice of adoption is inspired by the Australian Aboriginals. I first learned of this indigenous community at a Boeing Parapsychology Club meeting. A man spoke to the club about his time living within a tribe. He said this community believed they were so in harmony with the land and with each other, communication came in the form of thoughts more than anything else. I became immediately attracted to their natural way of life. Their philosophy reminded me greatly of Taoism, holistic medicine and natural remedies, such as homeopathy, aromatherapy, and acupressure closely related to utilizing natural elements at its rawest form to survive and thrive. Devastatingly, like the Native Americans, the Sacred Energy Life Force got interrupted, dishonored and disrespected by the civilized man which brought us to where we are today.
[130]Matheou, Demetrios. "The long walk home." The Telegraph. Telegraph Media Group, 01 Sept. 2002. <http://www.telegraph.co.uk/culture/4728661/The-long-walk-home.html>.
[131]Matheou, Demetrios. "The Long Walk Home." The Daily Telegraph UK September 2002.
http://www.telegraph.co.uk/culture/4728661/The-long-walk-home.html
[132]Flaherty, Jordan. "Saviors" Believe That They Are Better Than the People They are "Saving." AK Press. Thursday, January 05, 2017.
http://www.truth-out.org/opinion/item/38989-saviors-believe-that-they-are-better-than-the-people-they-are-saving
*Comments made by members on Social Media, including the Facebook Group: Adoption Truth and Transparency Worldwide Network

[133]Stephens, Tony. "Daughter dies with her story still incomplete". The Sydney Morning Herald. 15 January 2004. Retrieved 15 July 2007. http://www.smh.com.au/articles/2004/01/14/1073877902433.html ?from=storyrhs

[134]The Australian Women's Register: An initiative of the National Foundation for Australian Women (NFAW) in conjunction with The University of Melbourne. http://www.womenaustralia.info/biogs/AWE1185b.htm

*Doris Pilkington Garimara, novelist, is dead at 76. New York times. 21 April 2014 http://www.nytimes.com/2014/04/21/arts/doris-pilkington-garimara-novelist-is-dead-at-76.html?ref=obituaries&_r=0

*"Pot of gold at the end of the Rabbit-Proof Fence for Doris Pilkington Garimara AM.". Australia Council. Retrieved 29 May 2008.

*Dumas, Daisy (11 April 2014). "Doris Pilkington Garimara, author of Follow the Rabbit Proof Fence, dead at 76". Sydney Morning Herald. Retrieved 13 April 2014.

[135]Compiled by the Human Rights and Equal Opportunity Commission Reconciliation and Social Justice Library https://www.humanrights.gov.au/ https://www.humanrights.gov.au/publications/bringing-them-home-chapter-3

[136]Read, Peter (2006) [1st pub. 1982]. The Stolen Generations: The Removal of Aboriginal Children in New South Wales 1883 to 1969 (PDF). Surry Hills, N.S.W: New South Wales Department of Aboriginal Affairs. ISBN 0-646-46221-0. Archived from the original (PDF) on 20 August 2006. "Human Rights and Equal Opportunity Commission: Bringing Them Home: Part 2: 4 Victoria". AustLII. 1997. Confidential Testimony 253

[137]Confidential Evidence 689

[138]http://www.australia.gov.au/about-australia/our-country/our-people/apology-to-australias-indigenous-peoples

[139]The Stolen Generations "The Unfortunate Life of Bruce Trevorrow."

http://stolengenerations.info/index.php?option=com_content&vie
w=article&id=181&Itemid=162
'Stolen Generation Payout' *The Age*, Australia 2 August 2007; 'Test
for Stolen Generations Payout', *The Australian*, 28 February 2008
Gray, J, *Trevorrow v. State of South Australia* (No 5) [2007] SASC
285, Supreme Court of South Australia, Judgement of the Honorable
Justice Gray, 1 August 2007, para 110. This information on the
patient's history sheet was given by Mr. and Mrs. Evans, para 815.
[140]Today, this is called rehoming and a nationwide underground
epidemic in the adoptive parent community within the United
States. Adoptionland.org posts articles on the crisis.
https://adoptionland.org/rehoming-international-adoption/
[141]Roberts, J. "Stolen Generations Pioneer Bruce Trevorrow Dies."
The Australian, Online. June 21, 2008.
http://www.theaustralian.com.au/archive/news/stolen-
generations-pioneer-dies/story-e6frg6p6-1111116694899
[142142]

[143]http://www.abc.net.au/news/2013-03-21/gillard-delivers-
apology-to-victims-of-forced-adoption/4585972
[144]http://www.news.com.au/national/pm-moves-to-heal-the-
nation/story-e6frfkw9-1111115539560
[145]http://www.heraldsun.com.au/archive/news/transcript-of-kevin-
rudds-apology-to-forgotten-australians/story-e6frf7l6-
1225798255277
https://www.youtube.com/watch?v=3znXsldzMRo
http://news.bbc.co.uk/2/hi/uk_news/8531664.stm
https://www.youtube.com/watch?v=OAZywwaLR-o Kevin Rudd
apologizes on November 16, 2009 gave national apology in the
Parliament to the Forgotten Australians 500,000 children
http://news.bbc.co.uk/2/hi/asia-pacific/8361891.stm
[146]http://news.bbc.co.uk/2/hi/uk_news/8361025.stm
[147]Margaret pg. 75
[148]National Archives of Australia: Forced Adoptions History Project.
http://forcedadoptions.naa.gov.au/content/national-apology-
forced-adoptions

[149]http://www.abc.net.au/news/2013-03-21/gillard-delivers-apology-to-victims-of-forced-adoption/4585972

Prasanna, Sumithra. "The Murkier Side of Adoption" January 27, 2017 https://www.linkedin.com/pulse/murkier-side-adoptions-sumithra-prasanna?published=t

Adoption Profiteering in the US alone:

D'Arcy, Claudia. "Finally! Accurate Data on Profits in Adoption." Musings of the Lame: Adoption Birthmothers: Building Bridges to Adoptions Truths. February 27, 2015. "For over a year we have been able to say with confidence that the adoption industry brought in 13 billion dollars in 2013 based on an IBIS World market research report." "New Facts on Revenue and Profits in Adoption: Adoption services by agencies and facilitators alone are supposed to bring in over 30 million dollars in profit in 2015... ." *Just in the United States and this does not include adoption placements made by adoption attorneys.

http://www.adoptionbirthmothers.com/adoption-industry-profit-data-2015/

http://www.adoptionbirthmothers.com/wp-content/uploads/2015/02/62411-Adoption-Child-Welfare-Services-in-the-US-Industry-Report-2015.pdf

LINKS TO FBI, TRAFFICKING CASES, AND ADOPTION FRAUD:

Adoption Scams Bilk Victims, Break Hearts. (2006, August 28). Retrieved from https://archives.fbi.gov/archives/news/stories/2006/august/adopts cams_082806

Cooper, J. (2019, October 10). Politician charged in human trafficking adoption scheme. Retrieved July 23, 2020, from https://www.seattletimes.com/nation-world/nation/maricopa-county-assessor-indicted-on-adoption-fraud-charges/

Heisig, E. (2017, February 15). FBI raids Strongsville-based international adoption agency. Retrieved July 23, 2020, from https://www.cleveland.com/court-justice/2017/02/fbi_raids_strongsville-based_i.html

Kelly, D. (2019, January 11). FBI investigating Macomb County woman on suspicion of running unlicensed adoption agency, fraud.

Retrieved July 23, 2020, from
https://www.clickondetroit.com/news/2019/01/11/fbi-
investigating-macomb-county-woman-on-suspicion-of-running-
unlicensed-adoption-agency-fraud/
Kim, G. (2015, November 06). International Adoption's Trafficking
Problem. Retrieved July 23, 2020, from
https://harvardpolitics.com/world/international-adoptions-
trafficking-problem/
Mercer, R. (n.d.). FBI Adoption. Retrieved July 23, 2020, from
https://www.1idu.com/fbi-adoption/
Office of Public Affairs. (2019, September 05). Texas Woman Pleads
Guilty to Conspiracy to Facilitate Adoptions From Uganda Through
Bribery and Fraud. Retrieved July 23, 2020, from
https://www.justice.gov/opa/pr/texas-woman-pleads-guilty-
conspiracy-facilitate-adoptions-uganda-through-bribery-and-fraud
Oregon Dept of. (n.d.). Non-Departmental Adoptions. Retrieved July
23, 2020, from
https://www.oregon.gov/DHS/CHILDREN/ADOPTION/INDADOPTIO
NS/Pages/Background-Check.aspx
Reddit Discussion. (n.d.). R/PedoGate - IMPORTANT: Info regarding
Cleveland Killer that no one is talking about. Retrieved July 23, 2020,
from
https://www.reddit.com/r/PedoGate/comments/665yfv/important
_info_regarding_cleveland_killer_that_no/
Taylor/ABC7, S. (2017, February 15). Families stunned after FBI raids
adoption agency. Retrieved July 23, 2020, from
https://wjla.com/features/7-on-your-side/families-stunned-after-
fbi-raids-adoption-agency
Tracy Carloss, N. (2017, February 15). FBI searches debarred
adoption agency. Retrieved July 23, 2020, from
https://www.news5cleveland.com/news/local-news/oh-
cuyahoga/fbi-executes-search-warrant-for-european-adoption-
agency-in-strongsville
Unknown. (1970, January 01). Connect the dots ...CPS...
#PEDOGATE......On the grand scale of justice! Retrieved July 23,
2020, from https://outfortruthandjustice.blogspot.com/

ADOPTION TRUTH & TRANSPARENCY
WORLDWIDE NETWORK
For peer support plus more.

Adoption Truth connects domestic, intercountry and transracial adopted people, while expanding and advancing the discussion to include biological relatives and long-lost family members. Known for being one of the largest adoptee-led groups available on FB, you will also find a bird's eye view on the industry. Fellow members typically post the latest articles on adoption from local and global areas. As individuals and a collective, we also provide an environment of camaraderie intended to:

- Balance the professional field of adoption.
- Encourage the global discussion.
- Inform and empower families separated by adoption.
- Validate the vast experiences of adopted people.

Include your voice in the survey that will educate governments on the impact adoption has on the people, and find links at www.adoptiontruth.org.| admin@adoptiontruth.org.

Preserving Identity, History and Culture

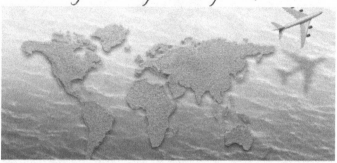

WWW.ADOPTIONHISTORY.ORG

NEXT EVENT:
ADOPTION TRAFFICKING AWARENESS SYMPOSIUM

RARE ADOPTION BOOKS FOR ADULTS CAN BE FOUND HERE:

ANGUS & ROBERTSON | APPLE | BARNES & NOBLE | BOL.DE |
BOOKMATE | CHINA | GOOGLE | INDIGO | KOBO |
MONDADORI | ODILO | SCRIBD | THALIA.DE | VIVLIO |
WALMART | 24 SYMBOLS

AMAZON (UNITED STATES) | AUSTRALIA | BRAZIL | CANADA
| DENMARK | FRANCE | INDIA | ITALY | JAPAN | MEXICO
| NETHERLANDS | SPAIN | UNITED KINGDOM

FOUND VALUE IN THIS BOOK?

The author would love to hear from you: review this book on the
profile page of the bookseller such as Amazon here.
Or send a note at
info@adoptionhistory.org.

***

IF YOU HAVE CONCERNS ABOUT THE BOOK,
Please feel free to email admin@adoptiontruth.org.